KILLING GROUNDS

The Saga of Encounters in Wild

KILLING GROUNDS
The Saga of Encounters in Wild

By
RAHUL SHUKLA

Photographs by
YOGESH KUMAR
I.A.S.

Foreword by
H. E. MOTILAL VOHRA
GOVERNOR U.P.

SIDDHI

SIDDHI BOOKS
IMPRINT OF
COSMO PUBLICATIONS
1995 INDIA

ISBN- 81-720-669-3

First Published 1995

Manufactured in India

Published by :
MRS. RANI KAPOOR
For SIDDHI BOOKS
Imprint of
COSMO PUBLICATIONS
For GENESIS PUBLISHING PVT. LTD.
24-B, ANSARI ROAD,
DARYA GANJ,
NEW DELHI-110002.
INDIA.

Typeset by :
MANAV COMPUTER HOUSE
DELHI-110092

Printed at :
Mehra Offset Press
New Delhi

Foreword

Motilal Vohra **Raj Bhavan**
Governor, U.P. **Lucknow, U.P.**

"Tiger, tiger, burning bright,

In the forest of the night,

What immortal hand or eye

Could frame thy fearful symmetry."

Thus wrote the great English poet William Blake about the tiger in 1794. The mysterious and the unknown has always excited human imagination. Dark forests have always beckoned those who love adventure. Wildlife has been a perennial attraction for conservationists, artists, poets, storytellers and alas! also for *Shikaris.* There is Kipling's lovable Bagheera, Jim Corbett's fearful man-eaters, Noronha and Ranjit Singh's beautiful photographs, the surrealistic and metaphysical prose of Peter Matthissen in search of the Snow Leopard and there are scientific treatise like the one by the redoubtable Shankhla on tigers.

Unfortunately, sometimes human beings prove to be the most dangerous beasts on Earth, bent upon the destruction of the life support systems of land, air and water and the entire biosphere, forcing varieties of fauna and flora to the brink of extinction.

Rachel Carson, the well known genetic-biologist wrote her famous book, 'The Silent Spring' in 1962 which became a trend setter and started the movement for preservation of ecology. The book warned us about the danger caused to wildlife by pesticides, fungicides and herbicides. In 1964, this book inspired John F. Kennedy, the then President of the U.S.A., to ban the use of D.D.T. This book set the tone for further explorations in the science of ecology dealing with the relation between living things and their environment.

Lord Shackleton wrote in his introduction to this book, "Ecologists are more and more coming to recognise that for this purpose man is an animal and indeed the most important of all animals and that however artificial his dwelling, he cannot with impunity allow the natural environment of living things from which he has so secretly emerged to be destroyed. Fundamentally, therefore, Miss Carson makes a well reasoned and persuasive case for human beings to learn to appreciate the fact that they are a part of the entire living world inhabiting this planet, and that they must understand its conditions of existence and so believe that these conditions are not violated". If so much of wildlife and birds and butterflies die, half the material for poetry will have perished.

Wildlife is indeed seriously threatened. The number of tigers is dwindling very fast. It is a tale of cruelty and cussedness that flesh and bones are being used in ointments, balms, wines and as aphrodisiac and they are being smuggled to China, Hongkong and Singapore. The habitat of elephants too which find mention in this book, is being destroyed. The heart rending tale of elephants in West Bengal forced by hunger to move to towns, and of pachyderms from Bihar to move to the forests of Madhya Pradesh is well known. Less known is how these gentle giants have been tortured and harassed during their flight.

I am glad that there are people like Shri Rahul Shukla and Shri Yogesh Kumar who are seriously concerned about the future of wildlife. This book is their love's labour. They are true friends of wildlife.

Introduction

K.K. Baksi
Additional Secretary

Ministry of Environment & Forests
New Delhi

I have looked with great interest through "Killing Grounds" by Shri Rahul Shukla illustrated with some excellent photography by Shri Yogesh Kumar.

The word Environment connotes a vast and complex subject, the contours of which are expanding to cover more and more areas, and the techniques and tools for the different sectoral and sub- sectoral aspects of environmental studies are also in a state of evolution. It is well-known that Nature and Wildlife are among the most important segments of Environmental studies, and works on these subjects are legion. But there has been a clear shift in emphasis from books on hunting and views of Wildlife from a somewhat exclusive and elitist line of thinking to one in which writers have been increasingly adopting an interventionist tone, and this is of course as it should be. But as we do have a large number of books available to us on Wildlife, it is necessary to judge this work from the standpoint of whether it has something to offer the reader in fields which have not received sufficient attention so far.

In my personal view, Shri Rahul Shukla has produced a very interesting work in which his deep sense of commitment to the preservation of Wildlife comes through very clearly. It makes interesting, even fascinating reading and brings home to readers who have no personal experience of studying Wildlife in its natural habitat, the stark realities which are confounding the whole situation. The first-hand accounts of poaching are of particular relevance for all those who vaguely know that such things do happen, but have no idea about how grim and horrible it all can be. Much of the information provided would be quite new to readers at large.

I would recommend this book to all lovers of Nature and Wildlife and hope that libraries will have copies available for their readers. I would also like to offer a special word of praise for Shri Yogesh Kumar, who has skillfully illustrated the text with some very imaginative photographs.

Preface

In the late evening of December 14, 1992, after a day's tiring work of photography, when Yogesh and I returned to Sonaripur rest house of Dudhwa National Park, the raucous birds of darkness had already come out of their hidden shelter. The night jars, owls and fruit bats screamed their hoary calls and kissed each other good day in sheer delight of the nocturnal dawn. We enjoyed the panorama of dusk and briefly paused at the entrance of the compound to notice their curious movements over the ground and on the terrace of the bungalow.

The birds presented a mysterious sight as they beat their wings in the still evening air while their big and small forms looked blurred in the concluding moments of twilight. They danced, leapt over one another, flitted, disappeared and reappeared in their frolicsome mood here and there in the premises of the forest bungalow.

We dumped our luggage in the *verandah.* There was no electricity in the rest house and no moon in the sky either. For the past two days, a major breakdown at the Palia power house had hampered the supply of electricity to the area. As I watched the light of the day merge with the blackness of the night, I was once again arrested by the curious phenomenon which the jungle presents during the miraculous switch-over from light to darkness at sunset. An aged caretaker unlocked the room with its cozy comfort and went back to his nearby home to fetch buckets of hot water. I lit a lantern and threw some dried stumps into the hearth to build a fire for warming the apartment. Then I placed a small kettle of water on the fire to brew some tea that would rekindle our tired spirits. Soon the caretaker was back with more water. A good wash gave us much relief from the day's fatigue. By now, the kettle was on the boil and soon we sat with steaming mugs of the ever-refreshing drink in our hands. To aid the recuperation were a couple of boiled eggs, bacon and some porridge.

We talked about the day's events in detail, precisely about the animals we had captured on film.

When our brief meal was over, I took out my diary and sat down at the table to scribble the highlights of the day's experiences. I had taken to this practice of writing a long time ago. Today I was in a mood to create an article for some magazine when Yogesh interrupted and said in his forthright manner: "Rahul, you have written a lot of articles in magazines and newspapers. Did you ever realise that the life of a newspaper is very short? It comes out in the morning and by afternoon it is thrown into the dustbin or used as waste paper. The same thing also happens to a magazine. Within a week of its issue, it becomes obsolete and meets the same fate as the newspaper."

"But the references are always preserved in a library, " I tried to present my argument. "No , definitely not in all the libraries," Yogesh replied categorically. "Only a few libraries preserve them and once they are dumped in the record room, it is a horrendous exercise to find exactly the issue you need to refer to. Besides, they are not kept for good. Old stocks are always sold to create space for new arrivals. Rahul, why should we not create some book together? We have already witnessed and lived through several exciting experiences and why should we not record them for posterity ?"

I had nothing much to say. He was right. A book never meets the fate of a magazine. Intellectual labour is never so wasted as it is in a newspaper. A book is an everlasting record of human knowledge. Finally convinced with this argument, I nodded in approval and there, in the remote alcove of a forest rest house, the concept of this book, which is now in your hands, was born.

Now that I have committed this book to paper, its foremost purpose is obviously game preservation and on this subject , I speak as a staunch conservationist and not as a hypocritic hunter. I say this because I am conscious of the fact that my first interest in wildlife had begun with the perspective of a hunter and a few episodes in the book pertain to the time when I held the gun in my hand. Yet, I consider myself mercifully free from the complex sentiments which have been much voiced in the complete volley of Indian hunting literature. In an interesting paradox, we find that almost every hunter, right from Victorian times, tried to project his personality as a supporter of conservation. The greatest butchers were the keenest supporters of any scheme of game preservation. They were the men with guns, out to save the animals, much as their counterparts with the woodcutter's axe may talk of saving timber. I fail to understand how a man can protect the animals he is deliberately out to destroy. The enthusiasm of these slayers can be undoubtedly attributed to their conceited double standards and cleverly selfish motives. The preservation of game was necessary and the stringent enforcement of law was imperative so the animals might multiply fast and then many more might be shot.

I have been associated with men for whom it was a passion to talk about conservation and game preservation while simultaneously remaining involved in the nefarious undoing of these very projects. Then it was a general trend to talk of deep affection and love for the animals one would invariably shoot. A few hunters even shed tears for the animals they continued to kill. Many of them talked of the pathetic depletion of a certain species yet they ate its steak with great pleasure. They were the true hypocrites, super representatives of classic pretenders and dissimulators.

Then there was a second category of men comprising a few genuine conservationists, but even they had taken up this subject quite late in their life apparently after having shot animals to their fill. Then the third category was of men who have either never shot an animal or have just temporarily shot, at some stage of their lives out of sheer necessity or circumstantial compulsion. I think I belong to this not very enterprising class.

In my tryst with providence, I am born in times which have in no uncertain terms witnessed the characteristic period of transition in respect to environmental consciousness. I have known of the times when just in a day, people had no compunction of shooting down any number of animals. Hunting was considered an honourable sport and the executioner of mighty beasts was regarded as a hero. I have witnessed a few glimpses of this great hunting era, although they were the last sparks of its final phase. Yet those were the days of hunters and the hunted, risk and glory, sportsmanship and bravery. I remember with gratitude the tense excitement of watching how the long line of twenty to thirty elephants surged about in the sea of grass in search of the striped predator and how the roars of the cordoned-off feline dominated the trumpeting of frightened elephants. Later the gay extravaganza with which the trophies were brought into the camps and the triumphant jambooree with which the accomplishment was celebrated.

Now hunting is looked down upon as an ignoble and cruel pastime. Hunters are no longer worshipped as heroes. The henchmen of these superhumans are unable to find a place for themselves in the community. On the other hand, present day society views them as villains, destabilizers and even anti-socials. These very hunters are held responsible for the near extinction of wild life. Now this contrast has so deeply set in, that the eventful era of hunting has been brought to a close. There can be no further contribution in this field.

My generation has witnessed an altogether new and supplemented aspect of this basically primeval instinct of violence. Although providing the basic subsistence for evolving mankind, it was both genuine and essential. Of course, with the development of civilization, hunting acquired a different meaning of pleasurable pastime, and still later, with the advent of the modern rifle, together with the large scale manoeuvres of ambitious trophy-seekers, the sport ceased to be a sport at all. On the scale of morality, it became controversial and degraded to the extent of being a crime. With the risk of some repetition, I say that I have been privileged to experience the swash-buckling element of enterprise in its obverse and opprobriousness in its reverse.

All this has happened under the shadow of an acute realisation that in the inequality of two forces engaged in the struggle, *viz*, man and nature, the latter cannot hold out for long. Nature has been so systematically attacked, subdued and thoughtlessly eroded by man's destructive instincts that countless animals and plants have already become extinct. Each loss impoverishes the environment and decimates the chances of long term human survival. We cannot continue the further unbalancing of our ecological system. This awareness has turned full circle and the general psyche of the masses has gone through a radical transformation, consequently conservation, ecology, pollution and preservation have become words of common vocabulary and a mature sense of responsibility seems to have set well in the majority of people. This far-sighted wisdom and the fear of circumstantial holocaust such as floods, droughts, earthquakes etc. has also culminated in the formation of strong public opinion against the primitive and cruel concupiscence of slaughter and deforestation, for there can be no ecology without biology and no biology without ecology.

Now, as I write this book in the early months of 1993, I feel concern about a small section of men who escape the fact that all life is interdependent and if we devour nature, nature will definitely devour us. These unabiding characters are the poachers. The tempest of their activities is still ravaging large areas in the Indian forests. It continues to destabilise nature's balance and prove a menacing threat to the primordial wealth.

Wildlife is vanishing at such a disastrous rate that prime areas where animals, in the recent past held an unquestionable sway, are now completely bereft of them. In my ancestral hometown of Mailani, sizeable herds of deer were regarded as the inevitable sight for a passerby. Hardly a day could pass without a sight or sound of a tiger. I am pained to state that at present, the area has become completely barren of its fauna. Nobody raises even a false alarm of a tiger's presence.

The political scene of our country is deeply complex. Many sceptics call India a functional anarchy. That is why, despite the knowledge of the consequential hazards, destructive activities continue unabashedly. It appears to be an irreversible automatic process which hardly leaves room for the remedy of this malady. I wonder why the government lacks the political will to solve these matters in a realistic manner? Petty and Selfish gains influence such crucial issues, and why does nobody want to take up cudgels against it ? Animals do not have a voice, they cannot create a forum or raise slogans against human plundering. They cannot vote for a party that would fight for their cause.

I have purposely written a chapter on the flourishing business of poaching. It exposes various devilish methods applied by poachers to achieve their ends. I hope that many of my readers after reading the inquisitions and expositions of whatever I know of poaching will not acknowledge the matter as amused pessimists, or remain a bystander, witnessing the eradication of India's wonderful heritage. If my accounts cast an influence on the feeling and sentiments of the new generation and motivate even a small percentage of the minority to assume the challengeful responsibility of the protection of their natural wealth, I would consider my efforts to be suitably rewarded.

And at last, to my mind, a jungle is always an enthralling place. You need not essentially be a hunter to derive a pang of thrill from it. In the interaction of different species, the magic of its melodramatic tunefulness never ceases to exist. The stimulation which mother nature inevitably imparts to an explorer and a genuine knowledge-seeker is never lagging behind. Although a rifle makes a man a more deadly predator than a tiger, after more than 25 years of association with the jungle, I feel qualified to state that it is a fallacy to say that a rifle will always help one to survive in an unhealthy predicament. In case of an erroneous shot, it is more liable to invite the wrath of a wounded animal and create trouble which otherwise would not have been there. And in the dark jungles and dense grasses where the visibility is less than a yard, a rifle is almost useless a defence. There, one's only means of protection are his sharp senses and an acute understanding of the jungle that warns one of danger beforehand, or at least at the right time.

At last, I lay no claim to my literary acumen and I am aware that I also lack the scientific training which could have otherwise helped me in the explanation of the works of many a qualified wildlifers. The photographs available in this book are the result of the assiduous labour of my companion Yogesh Kumar. Without them, it would not have been possible to make this book so colourful and glamorous. They suggest that photography is certainly a different outlet for man's atavistic passions for change.

The patience and self-control required to sit out for hours together under tiresome conditions to observe wild animals and then capture their elemental magnificence on camera is no less satisfying a reward.

LUCKNOW **RAHUL SHUKLA**

Acknowledgement

The urge to produce this book, was shared by my long-time associate Yogesh Kumar, who has been my constant partner in the long years of my jungle wanderings. I also got assistance from many people who supplemented my own observations, eradicated doubts and imparted invaluable information regarding the animal characteristics. I do not have adequate words to express the debt and gratitude I owe to these men. Numerous individuals, natives at first, then the forest rangers, guides, drivers, elephant handlers and camp managers have contributed in enabling me to realise the dream.

I am deeply indebted to M. Haider Mamman, the ex-professional hunter of Indian Shikar and Tours Pvt. Limited, New Delhi. He provided me with the initial idea to write this book. His company is a source of inspiration. He has now taken up the guiding profession and still brings great pleasure to those who accompany him on nature's excursions.

Yogesh and I have enjoyed the generosity of our well-wishers from the Indian Administrative Service. Prominent among them have been Mr. Anadi Nath Sehgal, Mr. B.N. Tiwari, Mr. K.R. Bhati, Mr. Prabhat Kumar, Mr. K.K. Baksi, Mr. N. Ravi Shankar, Mr. V.C. Pandey, my brother N.C. Bajpai and my father-in-law, Mr. B. K. Awasthi. They gave me a special kind of warmth and all of them remained always helpful and hospitable in the extreme. In particular, the constructive advise, assistance and concern of Mr. Jacob Thomas is genuinely appreciated, for he set the standards of excellence in being a friend, philosopher and guide. I am also thankful to my friends of the Indian Forest Service, namely Mr. D.V. Khatti, Director of Rajaji National Park, Mr. Shailendra Prashad and Mr. J.V. Sharma, Divisional Forest Officer of Dehra Dun and Saharanpur, who always took care to arrange for our stay in their respective areas. Mr. A.K. Singh, the Divisional Forest Officer of South Kheri Division, still remains our good friend and continues to cooperate in our field expeditions and provides us with the latest information.

Anand Sagar, a senior staff reporter of Gulf News, Dubai, freely gave me his time both professionally and personally. He took pains to read the initial draft of my manuscript written in almost indecipherable handwriting and offered his valuable criticism.

My grateful thanks also go to my wife Dr. Anita and her associate Dr. Nirmala. Both of them patiently converted the text into an immaculately written manuscript. My brother Anil Bajpai and my sister Dr. Chitralekha Verma bolstered my morale at crucial times. Yogesh's wife Dr. Suchitra Kumar provided ideal support and cooperation in making his task easier at every step.

Mr. Ratan Mani Lal, a senior editor at The Times of India, Lucknow, displayed exemplary tolerance to my requests and assisted me inspite of personal discomfiture.

We express our appreciation to Mr. Giriraj Shah of the Indian Police Service, who helped us in countless ways. Besides writing an introduction, he helped to give a shape to the manuscript and also found us a publisher.

And last, but not the least, we thank the Director of the Wild Life Research Institute, Dehra Dun and the Librarian of U.P. Secretariat who allowed us access to their libraries and often enlightened us with inspiring and profitable discussions.

My thanks are also due to the Editor of The Times of India, Lucknow, and Gulf News, Dubai, who kindly gave me permission to reproduce a number of articles entertained by their esteemed dailies. They were published under various titles esteemed dailies. They were published under various titles from time to time. In many cases, the title as well as the text of the articles have been changed, but the content remains the same as published in the papers.

Contents

1
The Elephantine Ordeal

The interminable time had clocked to 1 a.m., when Yogesh and I suddenly woke up together, all alert and cautious, listening to the unmistakable sounds of heavy bodies forcing their way into the water pond. The soft, squelching noises were succeeded by several popping notes being repeated from time to time. I listened intently and distinguished the sound of water being splashed and sprinkled by the animals over their bodies. I could infer that an elephant herd had arrived at the pond to quench its thirst and wallow in the water to beat the heat of the summer night.

A cool and pleasant wind blew over the pond and the surrounding jungle, maintaining complete silence, I carefully stood up on the *machan* and peeped down to see the herd. At a distance of over 200 yards across the pond, I sighted the elephants who had begun to enjoy the ablutions at leisure. They were entirely oblivious to, and undisturbed by, the close proximity of man.

It was the 15th day of our stay in Kishanpur sanctuary. Yogesh and I had arrived in Mailani on the 12th of June, initially with an idea of spending a couple of days wandering in the jungle and, if opportunity offered, we intended to record some observations of wildlife and then return to Lucknow as soon as the first showers of monsoon commenced. Normally in the Indian sub-tropical region, the rainy season starts in the middle of June but this year it had been delayed. It was the last week of the month and there were no sign of clouds in the sky. This delay in the rains had provided us an excellent opportunity to observe wildlife at water holes, as the intensity of heat was increasing everyday. The puny reservoirs of water were fast turning dry. In the extensive area of Kishanpur sanctuary, the reservoir of Jhati Tal was the only accessible source of water for wild animals. The concentration of a great variety of wildlife was available in this area, giving us an opportunity for a prolonged photographic session.

In the previous fortnight Yogesh had taken plenty of photographs in the sanctuary, clicking his camera at every available object. In this process he had completely exhausted the already inadequate stock of his films (mostly 200 and 100 A.S.A.) and now only a couple of 64 A.S.A. films were left in his bag. This film being very slow is absolutely useless for wildlife photography in night. Even if it is supported by a powerful flash light, it will fail to record even the slightest impression of the object. Night photography is a tricky business and one has to learn it by trial and error, in field conditions.

Almost a decade ago, when we were visiting the distant jungles of Bandhavgarh, now converted into a National Park, we had the stock of 64 A.S.A. films with us and we had tried to use a searchlight for the purposes of night photography. We had then taken along with us a 1.5 HP generator to operate the instrument. When we attached it with the searchlight in the dead silence of the jungle, it proved to be a very noisy contraption. We realized that it could better be utilised for intimidation and driving away the animals rather than attracting them, and despite so much of *bandobast*, our results of 64 A.S.A. reels had remained grossly disappointing.

Coming back to my present story watching from the *machan*, I looked at the rising moon. Its silvery and ethereal light had begun to flood the pond and the surrounding forest with a soft radiance, lending a mysterious and ghostly aspect to the immediate environment.

It was on Friday evening when Yogesh and I had decided to take our positions on the *machan*. We were enamoured with the idea of spending a night in the lap of mother nature where we wished to enjoy watching the secret world of the forest which essentially stirs into life in the blackness of the night. Towards dawn, after the vigilant observation of the entire night, we had also intended to avail the full benefit of early morning sunlight that would enable us to capture the panoramic beauty of the wild terrain. Although this particular time of the day lasts for a very short while, it is incomparably superb in its effect. The reflected light cast by the rising sun because of its 140 degree angle is natural, soft and soothing for a photographic adventure. The morning light imparts a luminous and lustrous tint to all objects of nature and makes them reveal their intrinsic colours.

Sitting on the *machan*, I enjoyed the sheer romance of the tranquil and serenely somnolent night. The stars flickered in their attempts to give off greater light while the moon floated up like a burnished globe with a beautiful rim carved out clearly for its travel across the heavens. I focussed my binoculars on the elephant herd and found the beasts involved in a gargantuan bathing ceremony. A few mighty looking males were seeking the deeper pool to delight in greater coolness while a few cows and their babies were just wallowing in the shallow waters. Summer season is unbearable for elephants because due to their massive bodies, the dissipation of heat becomes a big problem. The natural process of sweating does make them lose some of the heat but it is never enough to normalise their body temperature. In order to cool themselves they are always ready for a dip. In case water is not available in the vicinity and they are maddened by thirst, they have an in-built mechanism where they insert their trunk tips deep into their mouth and suck out water from their reserve pouch. It is an organ quite similar to that of cattle situated close to their throat inside their body. It holds 5 to 10 litres of a liquid which feels like thick saliva and in emergency situations, elephants also sprinkle themselves with this metabolic fluid to cool down their bodies.

I tried to estimate the number of animals, although it was not possible to count them exactly in the night, for many of them were moving haphazardly and moreover, the moonlight had also peopled the surroundings with fantastic shapes and shadows which gave the impression of the presence of a variety of animals. It appeared as if in the darkness, not only were many sambhars, cheetals, bears, jackals moving about, but even tigers and leopards were slipping in and out of the shadows. A rough count showed that the herd comprised more than 30 elephants. Apparently enough to be counted amongst them were 5 tusker bulls, 16 cows and around 10 calves. Their different sizes showed that they ranged from infant to sub-adult. All of them were seemingly in a mood for shenanigans, as I could make out by the euphonious sounds of their running behind each other in the shallow waters of the pond and spraying themselves with water.

A few elephants had already walked into the centre of the pond while a few were wallowing in the shallow waters, but still several of their companions stood scattered on the dry bank. They reflected a variety of moods: a few looked casual, a few were alert while some others just flapped their ear lobes, some looked so pensive and thoughtful as if they were bored with the burdens of their elephantine lives. At a distance of a little over one hundred paces stood another small bunch of young bulls, isolated from the rest and huddled together. They were swaying the flares of grass that were gripped in the tips of their trunks. This performance was being repeated at intervals with a prominent aim of driving away the hovering clouds of mosquitoes and insects feasting over their bodies.

The scene before us was a perfect realisation of a much cherished dream of a naturalist. The elephants, the moonlight, the pattern of shadows, the open sky, the brooding silence and the soft wafting breeze all were so beautiful and symphonic in their composition that we were mesmerised with the experience.

Suddenly my attention was attracted by a cracking sound. On the opposite bank of the pond, a dry branch of a tree had snapped with a sharp report. I changed postures and looked through my binoculars in that direction to locate the source of the sound. Gradually, a big shape emerged from within the shadows and as I focussed the glasses, the shape seemed to cover and fill the entire frame of the apparatus. There I spied a splendid tusker elephant standing at the outer rim of the forest. He was lustily feasting upon the branch he had just pulled down from the tree. He possessed a massive pair of symmetrical bars of ivory that looked gorgeously beautiful and gleamed pale and yellow in the ethereal radiance of the moon. In the diffused light, the tusker looked magnificent.

In the regions of the *Himalayan Terai* which I have travelled extensively, I had never seen an elephant with such long and beautiful tusks. He presented a stupendous sight and I had to admire his beauty. Long ivory tusks are very rare among Indian elephants mainly because the Indian forest végetation is low in calcium content whereas this ingredient is abundant in African fodder, thus the ivory is longer and stronger there. This elephant was certainly an exception and it reminded me of the flowery and romantic expressions of the Victorian ivory hunters who fondly addressed such elephants as the "grand patriarch", "the last survivors of the mighty mammoth" and "the sovereigns of pre-white India". Their writings show that these legendary animals were always surrounded by a dense ring of cows that would not let the hunter approach closer to him for a brain, heart or any other mortal shot. This tactic of protection adopted by the herd was chiefly responsible for his survival, and if by chance a hunter somehow succeeded in executing a shot, the wounded beast was not left to die on the spot. The shield of defence was so strong that the cow elephants were known to immediately lift up the old monster on a stretcher made collectively of their trunks and then supported by their fellow members, they were known to carry him deep in the jungles far away from the reach of the hunter. If wounded fatally, the tusker would at least be able to die a peaceful death and such grand trophies were almost never recovered. They were lost forever in the all concealing inner recess of the jungle and subsequently their ivory was always eaten up by porcupines. To my mind, this paradox exhibited the most befitting judgement of nature, an answer to the lust and greed of man. It was a well deserved punishment granted to any wanton trophy seeker by the power underlying all the material phenomena in the world.

So at last, there stood in front of us a mighty elephant, a rare sight we had so desperately wanted to photograph for a very long time but alas! as it always happens at such occasions, the light conditions were extremely bad. We also had such a bad film loaded in our cameras that we were utterly helpless to undertake any photographic adventure. The best thing advisable was to sit comfortably and record observations of elephant games. We had to wait for the break of the dawn, with a hope that the elephants would not depart before that. In fact, we were not at all happy to think of the second disconsolating probability.

After the passage of almost an hour, the very isolated bunch of three elephants gradually ventured close to the pond. They drank water, taking over 20 minutes, but the noticeable thing was that all this time while they stayed out of the water, none of them even tried to wet his feet, and after having their fill, they withdrew to the sandy bank and proceeded to romp in the dust. They filled their trunks with dust and sprinkled it over their heads and backs. I roved my binocular in the other direction to my left. On the bank there were many cows standing bogged down in the soggy soil and partially submerged in the shallow waters. They were busy caressing their calves, who were also half submerged.

For over an hour, the females and children bathed in the pond, blowing and splashing all the time. The hours quickly passed and the jungle cock nesting somewhere close to our *machan* rendered his rousing cry, indicating that the time was around 4 a.m. This call seemed to determine the routine of the elephant herd in a most uncanny way. I observed that all members of the herd ceased their activities and gradually walked out of the pond in strict obedience of nature's unexplained discipline. The grand patriarch who had uptil then done nothing significant but to prove himself a gourmand, turned and leisurely walked into the pond. At its periphery, he began to bathe, not caring to go in deeper and wallowed in the shallow waters. Lying on his back with his face upward, he coated his body with a thick layer of blackened mud. He rolled supinely for a few minutes. Then he straightened up, and suddenly, as if impelled by the sheer joy of being alive, he let out a loud trumpet blast of great triumph and exultation. It rang sonoriously through the stillness of night, travelled over the aisles of giant trees as if challenging the immense stretch of wilderness, the massive spread of sky, the world or even the limitless universe itself. The element of the intense savageness reflected in the vibrations of sound left us dumbfounded in acute admiration.

It was not long after this performance when the hazy creak of the false dawn appeared in the sky. With this first sign of morning, the great pachyderm finished his bath and leisurely walked out of the pond. He was completely bedraggled, then in a true regal elephantine manner, he slowly walked towards the jungle as if announcing to his fellow beings that the time for the washing ceremony was over and it was time for departure.

Thereafter, the herd followed him in strict obedience. In a single file all the animals drifted towards the jungle. The cows immediately assumed the duty of guarding their calves. The cows while moving are in a habit of ceaselessly caressing the young with their trunks. This precaution exercised by mothers does not permit the naughty youngsters to stray out of their sight and inadvertently separate from the herd.

It was thoroughly disappointing for us to watch the elephants slowly disappearing in the jungle. Dawn had already broken but before the light conditions could sufficiently improve for the purpose of photography, we were seeing the elephants disappearing into the woods. Yogesh felt morose and disgruntled and felt it was unfair on the part of elephants to have ditched him. We had kept awake the whole night waiting for this moment of light, and then when finally the desired time was just at hand, we were unable to photograph the elephants.

For sometime we remained in a state of indecision, the only consolation was that morning had dawned and stag herds were expected to arrive at the pond and they were also supposed to provide us with good picture material. It was better to photograph them and feel contented but in our heart of hearts, we were so charmed by the sight of the great patriarch that despite all odds we still wanted to photograph him. By a general surmise we thought that the elephants must not have gone more than a mile or so and if we hasten after them immediately, we were likely to find them in the neighbourhood. I left the decision to Yogesh, whether to go after the elephants or snap other animals? In keeping with what would have been my own decision, he chose to make an attempt on elephants. We hurriedly swallowed our breakfast while our Tharu guide bundled our paraphernalia and we proceeded on the trail of the elephants.

The shortage of time had limited our opportunity to analyse the outcome of our pursuit. The problem with elephants is that they are great wanderers and if today they are in this region, tomorrow they might be wandering 40 miles away from it, making it impossible to follow them. Hoping to catch them as quickly as possible, we did not plan our chase.

Needless to say, such activities are against all existing regulations of the park, but such things often take place, nevertheless.

Following an elephant herd on foot is a tricky affair. Anything is liable to happen when you are in elephant country, especially when one is going after them with a purpose. But despite this knowledge, I have a very soft corner for these big and noble animals. When I consider the hardships I always have to endure in following the trail of a tiger or leopard, I conclude that following the herd of elephants is comparatively a tame sport. They invariably give away their position by the noise they make in undergrowth while feeding, and then it becomes a relatively simple matter to stalk them from the favourable direction of the wind. If one can avoid stepping on dead leaves and twigs that crackle to betray the stalker's position, one can reach within a very short distance of them and manage some good photographs.

Bordering the pond for a couple of furlongs, the area was clothed with a species of a tall flowering grass. The Jhati Tal area is full of this particular variety. The grass attains a height of nine to ten feet at places and its roots sustain life on sub-soil moisture. The top of the grass is ornamented with a beautiful blossoming stem which closely resembles the flowering heads of sugarcane but when in their prime, they assume a greater length and much finer texture.

It was early morning and the droplets of dew which had collected overnight on the fine strands of these flowerheads glittered resplendently as the rays of the rising sun delicately danced over them. The effect was a gemlike appearance of the slender fronds and rewarded the country with a vision of beauty and peace. This picturesque scenario entirely belied the danger that threatened us in the grass.

Yogesh and I slowly entered the grass. Having walked for a couple of hundred yards inside it, we realized that due to its height, the visibility inside it was not up to the mark. The stems had grown to such a height and in such thick profusion that we could not see more than two yards ahead. It was astonishing to find that though the elephant herd had gone through this way, very little grass had been crushed. Even the bent stems were now rapidly resuming their upright position, so we had to constantly part them with our hands in our efforts to move fast.

Walking through this type of grass jungle is a very dangerous affair. We had no weapons in our hand to guard against a surprise attack of any dangerous beast. A tiger or a leopard that rested in such cool and shady places could find easy targets in us, so we had to continue our advance with utmost precaution. A slightest relaxation of caution on our part could easily plunge us into a dire disaster.

This realization that we were exposed to multiple dangers was very genuine but it had come to us so late that it was hardly of any pragmatic utility. On the other hand, it could only be a negative contribution that would make us uncomfortable and demoralise us. The simple reason was that we had already travelled so far in the jungle, it was not possible to abandon the trail at this moment. Even if we decided to go back under any apprehension, it would have again meant a long travel through the grass and in this act of withdrawal there was no surety that we would not encounter danger on our way back. So it was better to press on, or try to reach the regular Sal forest and from there choose a suitable route to travel back to our camp. I discussed this proposition with Yogesh and was glad to know that he was thinking on similar lines but being impetuous in his inclinations, he appeared more keen to photograph the pachyderms rather than terminate activity at this point. I finally surrendered to his will.

The sun had risen high in the heavens. It's sword like rays were beating down upon us mercilessly. The atmosphere all around us was intensely quiet. The stillness of air and the humidity of swamp grass along with the scorching heat had made our walk difficult. We were feeling tired and thirsty and sweat covered our bodies so profusely that were dehydrated. What in the beginning we had presumed to be a simple affair, had now gradually become a tough proposition. The ordinary routine of a naturalist had now transformed itself into an elephantine task.

The atmosphere was absolutely still, we could hardly feel our own breathing. The heat had become devastating. We did not know how much distance we had covered in the grass but by an approximate guess, I somehow felt certain that we had covered more than five or six miles through the jungle. Having walked for almost a *furlong* more we found the grass to be thinning down and finally ending, to give way to a clearing. As the waist high grass cleared, we emerged out of it to be welcomed by the beautiful view of two distinct jungle trails running parallel to each other on our both sides at a distance of half a kilometer.

A vantage point offered us a vision of long distances to our right, left and front, and we were disappointed to notice that there was absolutely no sign of the elephants anywhere in all the directions. Our efforts seemed to have become an exercise in futility, and our spirits plummeted even as we looked at a great trail of jungle stretching before us. Thirsty and tired as we were, we had no more energy left to go after the elephants who could be anywhere in the dense jungle. I looked at the ground. The elephant trail was very conspicuous and we could still have followed it without any difficulty. But our Tharu guide was unwilling to carry on. He had given up all hopes of relocating the whereabouts of the elephants. We stopped at a point to drink whatever little supply of water was left in our bottles while the Tharu was busy with arguments and counter-arguments, displaying his strong reluctance to follow the trail. And at last, he could convince us. Consequently we decided to drop the trail and call it a day.

In going back home, the only advisable way was to retreat through the Sal jungle. There the undergrowth was not expected to be dense and we were not supposed to encounter the problems we had faced so far in the grass. Imagining that it was enough adventure for a day, we turned and walked towards the forest trail. However, we had absolutely no realization that our major share of misadventure was not to be over soon, and much more of it was there in the offing for us.

We had barely travelled a few hundred yards when, while crossing a small clearing, I struck the spoors of elephants once again. Here the ground had been deeply ploughed by mighty plate-like feet. There were both old and new spoors, criss-crossed by many deer and antelope tracks. I scanned the ground and recognised some new and very fresh spoors. These seemed to have been made only that very morning. At first, I thought that these tracks were made by a different herd of elephants, but our Tharu guide declared that they were made by the same herd we were following since the morning. He pointed to several tracks identifying them as being of those elephants whom we had exclusively wanted to photograph. It was their charm which had made us undertake this adventure. The tracks confirmed that while moving through the grass, the elephants had abruptly changed course, to approach the nearby grass and subsequently, their journey had been through this route to enter the trail. The reason for this act was obviously the growing heat of the day. The sun blazed relentless in the sky. It had become unbearable for the animals and soon, the animals had been compelled to seek cool and shady shelter which they needed for a good sleep in the hot hours of the day.

This chance finding of tracks once again boosted our spirits. I broke open a lying dung ball and felt for its warmth; it was fresh and we felt sure that at least this time the elephants would not be able to outdistance us.

The country we were passing through was completely dry, but still the growth of vegetation was dense. Under the heat of the sun, at several places the grass clusters had turned yellow. They were so dry that a careless throw of a cigarette butt could have set the forest on fire for miles. We walked on the trail in a single file and within a couple of minutes we found ourselves negotiating our way into another block of the jungle. As I viewed the heavy forest, my spirits sank low. Indeed, it was truly dense and absolutely wild country, hardly visited by man. I would never have gathered sufficient confidence to traverse it on my own had we not been accompanied by the Tharu guide. To add grimness to the wilderness, no annual grass burning had been carried out in this area and, thė undergrowth that largely comprised lantana and thorny shrubs had become compact and massive. The closely-set giant Sal trees that grew in profusion, towered over us. Their canopies obstructed the passage of light and cast deep and dark shadows on the ground. A strange kind of twilight seemed to permeate the atmosphere. Small swift birds flittered here and there in the undergrowth. The light conditions had become extremely bad and we thought the trailing was of no use as, even if we met the animals, we would not at all be able to photograph them. The day's exercise had been highly strenuous and all we could do was to curse the day and regret having chosen to follow the wrong animals at a wrong time and in a wrong place.

We were standing in the midst of wilderness. There were no forest roads, footpath or even a game trail in sight. Because of the jungle's density, it was essential to keep guard in every direction as at present, the elephants were certain to be dwelling somewhere in the jungle and they could come out from anywhere. So we began our journey towards the camp. We tried to keep all our faculties alert. This trail seemed to contain all the thrills for the liking of big game hunters who were known to pursue their quarry regardless of the land terrain and the hardest of the conditions. Our Tharu guide was excellent in his ways, displaying utmost confidence in himself like the classic tracking companion of his old master, he walked without stirring a leaf. I rated him as highly capable and intelligent and a pastmaster of his special craft. Throughout this trail, he had repeatedly proved his expertise, efficiency and talent. He was straining his ears and trying to pick up even the slightest of sounds as we moved further into the jungle.

Then I suddenly heard a sound that I had so long been hoping to hear: it was the unmistakable scraping sound of a branch being torn down from a tree. All three of us abruptly stopped in our tracks. Then the sound was followed by a swishing noise as the green leaves were stripped from the bough by a giant's ruthless destructiveness. It indicated that an elephant was engrossed in feeding. The sound continued for about five minutes and it seemed to be coming from behind us. This was shocking: we had never expected to encounter an elephant from our rear. Feeling quite certain about the direction, I instantly turned to locate the place of its origin. As I looked back, I met with the shock of my life. A cold chill ran down my spine when I saw that barely ten metres away to my left stood a cow elephant with a calf sprawled in between her legs. Mercifully, her eyes were closed and she appeared to be sleeping and I could see her trunk hanging loosely. Suddenly Yogesh tapped my leg and pulled gently my trouser. As I turned to note his signal, I found him lying prone on the grass. He signalled me to fall flat on the ground. I instantly obeyed him, accomplishing a similar performance. Then he slowly raised his fingers and pointed to the right and there was another nerve shattering sight. Hardly twenty paces away from us there were standing two cow elephants.

They were quite close to each other and also appeared to be-sleeping. I froze where I was. It was the most unexpected and disagreeable situation for us. We could not dare raise our heads or even try to hide ourselves in the undergrowth, for the slightest movement on our part could betray our presence to the elephants.

Raising my head a little, I slowly scanned the ground to ascertain if there were any more elephants around. Besides these three in view, we could see none. Due to nervousness and excitement, I started sweating. I could clearly hear the uncomfortable beat of my heart pounding hard against my ribs. The realization of the mistake that we had committed, made us think about the misfortune that could befall us. I am sure that even the most ardent and the dare-devil ivory-seekers of the past would never have lived through the kind of situation we were now facing. And even if they had, by chance, they would have essentially been armed with heavy calibre rifles to protect themselves, whereas the only extra apparatus we had in our hands were the cameras and their lenses. In fact, we had inadvertently walked right into the middle of the herd without having the faintest idea of the danger we were going to encounter.

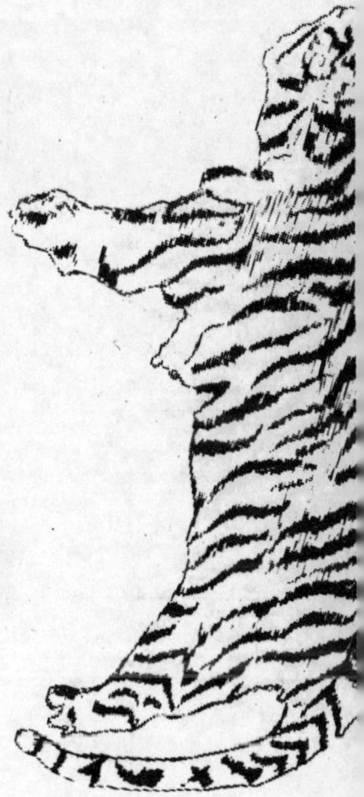

Despite all the odds I could not help wondering at the innocence of elephants. They were sleeping contentedly, completely indifferent to human presence in their close proximity probably because there was no perceptible wind to carry our scent to them. The hottest hour of the day had commenced and that is why the elephant herd, after having entered the forest, had come to an abrupt halt. A pleasant change in the temperature had quickly lulled them into a delicious slumber,

their customary noon siesta. This was responsible for tracting us so deep into the jungle as, while doing so, we had been completely unable to detect any sound that could have indicated the whereabouts of the elephants.

The time was around 10 a.m. I was certain that most elephants of the herd were sleeping and the odd sounds of feeding that I had heard moments ago had naturally come from some insomniac member of the herd. But I was positive that this awake elephant was stationed at a distance that was not less than hundred to hundred fifty metres away from us and in between, there was a lot of dense cover. So, luckily, we not expect to be seen by him so soon, but still the situation was grim and discouraging. None of us could muster up sufficient courage to embark upon any kind of manouvre to get out of this dreadful situation. Among the many thoughts that passed through my mind was one when I tried to imagine the way elephants think. In an elephant country it is highly advisable to know something about the working of the elephant's mind as it enables a naturalist to anticipate his actions and reactions under different circumstances. But this gift of sixth sense is certainly not possessed by all wildlifers and I did not wish to delude myself in believing that I could do what I could not. There was no harm in doing this, the advantage was that I could make out the respective spots in dense covers where the remaining elephants might have presumably stationed themselves, planning all the while a strategy to chart a probable route for our escape.

Meanwhile, Yogesh whistled softly to me indicating something new. My attention was caught by dull movement of a heavy body crashing down everything in the way which obstructed its passage. I whistled back to acknowledge his signal and waited for the beast to put in an appearance. Soon in front of us at a distance of thirty yards, the bushes parted and revealed the massive bulk of a slate grey body. This was a tusker elephant but not exactly the one we had wanted to photograph. He came into the open and halted for few seconds. Then he shook his head to drop the dry twigs from over him. His beautiful, symmetrical ivories gleamed and flashed for a brief second and releasing a hollow sound from his trunk, he slowly trudged away from us into the density of the jungle.

We lay there prostrate on the ground in whatever scanty grass cover was available while the elephants around us stood immovable like pre-historic rock: solid, indestructable and eternal. We were at a loss to decide as to how to react. The very sight of this mighty elephant had frozen the blood in our veins. Scared out of our wits, we scarcely dared to breathe. Seconds melted into minutes and the minutes dragged like hours as we tried to exercise the utmost patience to maintain silence. Due to overwhelming fear and a sense of tremendous insecurity in our minds, our nerves were on the verge of cracking. The anxiety had turned my brain cold and even my senses felt temporarily paralysed. We could not move at all from our miserable positions for the fear that even a puny initiative on our part could awaken the elephants. It is a matter of general knowledge that neither man nor beast likes to be awakened suddenly while enjoying a peaceful siesta. I think only those people who have experienced it would better appreciate the extent of the flurry, bustle and agitation which ensues on such occasions and then the moments that follow. They are a genuine cost paid for the fault of disturbing the mighty slumbering beasts.

The stillness was intense and we had perspired profusely because of the high excitement. This phenomenon had already increased the chances of our presence getting detected easily by the elephants who have a superbly developed olfactory sense. Even the slightest whiff of air carrying the faintest of our smell could not escape from being registered by their supersensitive nostrils, so it was primarily and absolutely essential for us to mask our body odour. One may become sceptical

and say what nonsense am I talking about! You may question as to how can man possibly succeed in such an effort? But in those disastrous moments, it was essential to do so and the only possible way for the suppression of human scent was to coat our bodies with elephant dung or at least smear it on our clothes or on the exposed parts of our bodies.

The balls of elephant dung, both old and fresh, were lying scattered around us. I broke open one ball, and, smearing it on my hands and clothes, gestured to Yogesh to make free use of it, but keep his movements restricted while doing so. It was a highly unpleasant task but, I was convinced that it was the only possible answer to our predicament, to avert a catastrophe.

The very thought of getting trampled under the columns of mountainous flesh was extremely horrendous to bear and then, when the worst was liable to happen, the smelly task hardly looked ungainly or awkward to us.

The second imperative was to remain immobile, and we were practicing this after becoming aware of the surrounding elephants. Even straightening up or squatting would have been disastrous for us as the slightest movement involved in doing so would have paralleled an earthquake. It could perhaps be conceived by any odd elephant who happened to be awake and looking in our direction. We had to remain completely still and also fully prepared to remain in that position for a length of time. It could be anything from one hour to four or even more. We kept lying in that cramped position counting minutes and repeating supplications, waiting for the elephants to migrate elsewhere.

Fortunately, the wind had been almost dead so far, which was in our favour. It seemed most likely that by noon it would gain some strength and make the situation truly dangerous.

Elephants are short sighted beasts so we had the consolation, that their myopic vision could not detect us.

The marks of strain and tension had appeared on the faces of my friends. The only thing to do was to depart from the scene with the least possible delay, for it was now getting around an hour since we were cramped and immobile, feeling the mounting pressure of ordeal. My patience was giving way, so I decided to be courageous and put an end to the unpleasant situation. I made a thorough inspection of the surroundings to make sure whether the elephants were genuinely sleeping and whether it was all safe to move on the ground. I tested the wind direction but it showed no movements and finally, with a resolute decision, I began my full hearted attempt to clear out of that dreadful place. I patted Yogesh on his shoulder to follow me. The Tharu guide had already begun to move. All three of us crawled slowly in the reverse direction, hopefully on the very track we had recently followed to come here. We avoided passing through any of the dense growth, for we did not know where the other elephants of the herd were sleeping and we did not wish to bump into any one of them. Carefully, we continued the retreat, stealthily negotiating from an unpleasantly close range of sleeping cows and conscious of the fact that our manoeuvring involved a grievous personal danger. We had to accomplish this, for our very survival depended upon that. Despite my honest attempt to escape, I admit that the outcome of this exercise, at least to my mind, was thoroughly unpredictable, but I pressed on, followed by my companions in complete understanding. Crawling on a forest floor can be a daunting task, but this was more cumbersome for us as we also had two cameras with us. To avoid any metallic sound from emanating in our exercise, we took a camera each and moved only after we had placed it an arms length ahead of us. This way, we covered more than twenty yards in the first stroke and then in a scrap of a small cover, we stopped to take some rest. My whole body had

begun to ache, and my hands were feeling terribly weak. My mouth was dry and my tongue had swollen with thirst. I am not selfishly describing my own reactions, all of us were experiencing more or less the same feelings.

After a brief pause, I was again getting ready to resume the crawl when I heard a series of rumbling sounds coming from a close by bush. These distinct sounds occur in an elephant's stomach in the process of digestion. This was disturbing. Some elephant was certainly there, standing hidden from our eyes. I crawled back inside a clump trying to master my mad urge to stand up and run away as fast as I could.

I did not know that our Tharu guide had already fallen prey to this thought. In sheer desperation and much because his inability to endure the imparingly bad tension, he got up foolishly and shouting like a hysterical person, ran out and before I could stop him, he had dashed away like a sprinting cat into the density of jungle.

At first, we thought that our end had come at last in a most ignominious way. But later, this foolish act interestingly turned out to be a positive gamble as it quickly brought an end to the continuing stalemate.

The elephant baby who was sprawling between its mother's legs was first to jump into life. He exhibited a panic stricken shock and began to dance around his mother with his tail fully erect. The mother also did likewise, answering the call of her child in a earpiercing scream, apparently to defend him from the unseen danger. And then both of them ran fast inside the jungle.

Just at that moment I felt that the whole jungle had become alive with activity. Various types of sounds rose from the unseen elephants, indicating that a kind of general confusion had spread amongst them. Their giant bodies swayed through the heavy growth and in subsequent moments I could hear the herd crashing through the density of the jungle. Disturbed elephants were trumpeting loudly for no apparent reason. The earth seemed to quiver and tumble under the mighty pounding of the great columns. Twigs, trees and branches were knocked down, uprooted and crashed against the force of their panic stricken flight. The forest resounded with their violent movements. We lay flat on the ground where we were listening to the terrific commotion that was slowly fading away as the distance of the fleeing elephants increased from us.

After approximately two minutes, which seemed like eternity, the uproar appeared to be subsiding. The stampeding elephants had undoubtedly taken to a marathon run. Once outraged in this way they would go for miles before they stopped. Then, after some time all sounds quietened down and within a span of five minutes, there was almost no audible sound not even a faint whisper to catch our attention.

We had lived and survived through a harrowing experience. The incident had been bad enough and we were feeling quite paralysed by fear to be capable of reacting. We got up slowly and trying to keep the necessary patience, we slowly walked out of the jungle. The sun blazed in its full glory and although we were acutely conscious of thirst and exertion, still it was relief to feel the openness. The shock caused by the stampede was slowly being felt. We did not speak but again began to traverse through the grass. Providence was kind to us, for here we unexpectedly came across our Tharu guide. He had heard the spate of screams and thinking that we had been killed in the stampede, he was now coming back to collect our remains. He grinned and ran happily on seeing us and we thanked the Almighty for providing him to us to cross the wilderness. These tribals seemed to have a compass in their nose. As a rule, they never forget the way, the sun, stars, the moon, trees and land terrain all of these *featerkeri* seem to help them. I think it is largely because of their closeness to nature whereas the senses of a town-bred man are dulled and weakened in this regard by the humdrum of city life.

We reached the campsite late in the afternoon, hungry, thirsty and excessively tired. A cold bath and a long gulping drink, followed by richly sugared milk served us as the best thirst quencher. We took a greedy meal and as we lay down, we immediately fell asleep.

Towards the evening our eyes opened. Darkness had gathered in the sky. The distant chuckling of a scavenging hyena was shattering the stillness of the evening with its maniacal laughter. The abominable sound floated by sometime, then died away in the parched countryside. They were shortly succeeded by a howling chorus of night hunting jackals. We sat in the *verandah* of the rest house and enjoyed glasses of sundowner while listening to the queer noises of a jungle night. We were pleased to be alive after an ordeal which was as scary as it was unforgetable.

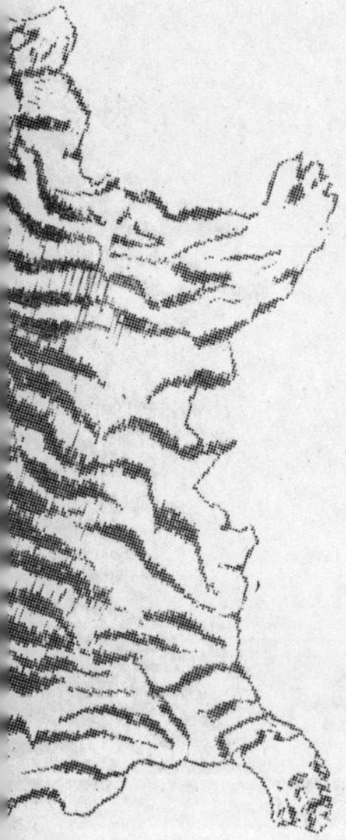

As there was no electricity in the rest house, the attendants had built a small bonfire in the courtyard. As I observed its glowing embers, my mood became reflective, going back to the days of our early association.

A longish time had passed since Yogesh and I had first met in Allahabad University's A.N. Jha hostel. We had many interests in common, and the most prominent among them was the passion for wildlife. Within moments of starting our first conversation, we became good friends. With the passage of time, our companionship intensified and I could foresee a budding photographer in him. Because of this hobby of his, we subsequently embarked upon many an adventure and on more occasions than one, his overzealous approach landed us into sticky mud, quite literally.

But, it is only such a devil-may-care attitude which always

makes one thrust forward and ultimately obtain rich rewards in life. The book in your hands is an account of a few such excursions and it may be of interest to keen wildlife researchers and also to those who have had a lesser share of experience than I have had.

2
Early Days

"A ... was born just before midnight and I shall never forget how his first infantile cries were mingled with the howling of jackals."

A.I.G.R.

It has been for more than the last twenty-five years that I have lived in close association with the world of nature. I ascribe this credit to my maternal family which boasts of protracted and deeply ingrained roots in the Terai Region of district Lakhimpur Kheri which falls in the province of Uttar Pradesh in northern India. The district borders are contiguous with Nepal in the north. Being situated at the base of the Himalayas, a number of rivers and rivulets criss-cross the territory. In the course of their journey to the Bay of Bengal, they meander through the Terai and beautify it with an evergreen ambience. The main rivers of the area are Ghaghra, Sharda, Suheli, Gomti, Mahona, Katna etc. Nearly twenty percent of the district's area is covered by evergreen tropical forests. The internationally famous Dudhwa National Park covers twelve per cent of the aforesaid area. It is located across the Sharda in the north division of Kheri District. It contains one of the finest wilderness of north India. In the times of pre-independence, this region offered one of the most spectacular wildlife sights of the Terai.

It was a feast for the eyes to see the great herds of cheetal, nearly a thousand of them, bounding through the forest over the ash of the freshly-burnt undergrowth, or the herds of gregarious swamp deer splashing through an expanse of water, or the colonies of black bucks taking a flight in steeping and floating action.

A discordant and intermittently spaced chain of my ancestral villages, lies in and around this primeval wilderness. It starts right from the south division and goes across the Sharda, and continues upto the north division to the proximity of Dudhwa Park. One settlement amongst them is known by the name of Larti. It is situated in the south division of Kheri. It was actually from this point that my interest in nature had originated.

The village has an interesting history of more than ninety years. In the early years of this century, my great-grandfather had bought nearly five hundred acres of virgin land from the erstwhile Raja of Khutar which was then a princely state of Shahjahanpur district. This remote area was called Gadaula in the Government record. There was no agricultural development in this region and the wild animals roamed everywhere. Notorious gangs of dacoits lived in the vicinity. A multitude of poisonous snakes together with the dreaded diseases malaria, filaria, and occasional outbreaks of epidemics like cholera, jaundice and typhoid regularly claimed a substantial toll of human lives.

My grandfather was undaunted by these hazards. He got over hundred acres of land cleared of vegetation and converted the land into a profitable farm.

This village of Larti lies four kilometres to the south-west of Mailani railway junction and at an equal distance from Kishanpur sanctuary that falls across the railway line in the north and forms an integral part of the Dudhwa National Park. Although the comforting amenities of civilisation have crept up in the township of Mailani, yet this village still retains its primeval character. A lush vegetation of thickly-set Sal forest surrounds it from all the four directions. This is a landscape of huge trees and creepers punctuated by reed, *ekra* and elephant grass. It is also interspersed with small and big water ponds. At present, the wanton poaching of timber and wildlife has left it largely bereft of its natural wealth. Thanks to the efforts of forest officials, some pockets of dense woodlands still remain intact. Despite this, it has become divested of wild life. The surroundings are enough to remind an onlooker that in the recent past, this country must inevitably have been a prime habitat for the wild ungulates and their predators.

A vast expanse of cultivated fields starts from outside the very edge of the enclosing forest. These days, approximately two hundred square acres of land is being cultivated in Larti and throughout the year, it's sizeable portion remains largely laden with the basic commercial crop of sugarcane. One can see their swaying fronds spread all over the farm land from one end to the other. They reach up to the last square yard of the forest rim and at places they even penetrate for a couple of hundred yards inside the jungle. The long stems of cane crop are thickly set. They clasp and interlock each other so tightly that they make the crop an essentially dense growth. The nature of sugarcane helps to serve the wild life as another extension of their habitat, besides the regular forest. They take it as an expansion of their natural grassland and as its outcome, the sugarcane crops always remain infested with wild animals. Wild boars and tigers are specially partial to the comforts of this crop. They inevitably dwell in it as soon as they are grown enough to offer them adequate concealment.

Larti has a typical beauty of nature. I can still remember every aspect of the bygone days with a nostalgic vividness. The elliptical headtops of the closeby Kakrahi village rising against the background of the towering foliage of Sal trees, the rioting colour of wild rose, verbena and jungle lily and the beauty of surrounding forest, was enlivened by a variety of wild life. A small water pond lay a mile away from Larti. It was surrounded by riverine flora, mainly arrowhead reeds and blade grass. It was a haven for feathered game. The wild ungulates also frequented this marshy patch. Often in the nights, while lying in the *verandah*, of my ancestral house, I heard the swamp deer calling each other and the bugling of swamp stags. At times, they were supported by the rutting bray of sambhar or the hoarse falsetto calls of cheetal males.

I also recall the Katna river, that flowed three miles to the southwest of the village inside the teak forest plantation. It crept up silently concealed beneath the surface growth of water-hyacinth that rose up in thick masses. It was heavily loaded with a variety of fish and here brilliantly coloured kingfishers flittered. To catch them up and down the water and trees and the unconcerned groups of butterflies trailing lightly from their gaudy wings flitted out from the glooms of Sal, to dance over the muted pristine space. The lilting crow of the jungle cock and the clarion call of peacock resounded on the banks of the river at all hours of the day. These sounds were recurrently stamped by the anxious staccato barks of a lone *kakar* who had made up his residence near a *jamun* tree that grew on the bank of the Katna river. The creature habitually kept a watch for the bloody customers of the jungle and never failed to warn his colleagues about the arrival of some carnivorous danger, and, above all, at nightfall, I recall fireflies that flickered and flittered with their tiny lamps, infiltrating the branches of trees to give them a gleam of a star-studded greenery of fire.

This haughty country gave me a splendid sense of freedom and space. Its pastoral fantasia held an irresistible charm for my imagination. I was fascinated by its savage yet innocent nature and specially by the numerous sounds of diurnal and nocturnal creatures. They lent a magical enchantment to the atmosphere. They were tempting and inviting enough to draw me deep into the lap of nature. As my intimacy with the surroundings increased and I acquired a knowledge of different jungle blocks, I found that apparently unattached jungle sounds had a rhythm of their own. The chirps, squeaks, cracks, jabberings, howls and yowls that meant little or nothing to an uninitiated watcher, conveyed a definite meaning to me. I found that I was no longer confused by the similarity of different jungle game trails and the complex nature of vegetation. This wilderness turned into my favourite haunt and latter became my foremost playground. In subsequent years, I zeroed in on these jungles for a lot of my multifaceted adventures.

A stroll in them was itself a romance with nature. The tranquil landscape harboured many a dignified and bounder killer beasts. Looking respectable from outside, they were quite inhospitable in their interiors. As an immature boy, I fully intended to accept its insidious challenges. In the heart of these woodlands, I have spent innumerable hours in search and observation of wild animals. In them, I have hunted deer, wild boars and other lesser game. I have tracked the trails of big cats. I have waited for them at their favourite haunts. I have watched them and also tried to photograph them in their true feline regal glory.

My maternal ancestors had settled down in this region four generations ago and since then, a tradition of hunting had originated in my family. It was born out of the sheer necessity to resist the plundering of the marauding beasts, for in the darkness of the nights, great herds of antelopes and deer regularly came out of the forest and demolished whole fields of barley, maize, wheat etc.

The wild pigs were an especially incorrigible nuisance. They dug up potatoes and peanuts and often damaged a greater quantity than what they could actually consume. The pragmatic solution to this problem lay in the elimination of these raiders. The farmers were troubled, for the local supply of wildlife was so great that bags of bullets were emptied upon them, yet the animals continued to pour in. Hunting also continued as an effective remedy to the menace. Gradually, with the passage of time, it developed into the principal recreation of my family. Many enthusiastic members took this sport as a good outlet to display their prowess and when, as a member of the fourth generation, I visited this village in the early sixties, I found that the pretext of crop protection was not valid for this thoughtless, illegal execution. Every kind of wildlife was being relentlessly eliminated. I cannot recall a single day in Larti when we were not treated with some kind of game recipe. On our dining table hog deer steaks in the morning, rabbit soup at night, peahen *kababs* breakfast and spotted-deer fillets lunch constituted a part of our usual menu.

This village was managed by a distant collateral of my family, and still continues to be so. He stands as an uncle of mine in relationship. Now an old man, he lives there as the last feudal vestige of the bygone times. What I liked most in him were his dramatic ways to impress people. He reflects a potential gust of force in his personality. This element is so innately proficient and so characteristically incorporated into his self that it lends him with a virtual blaster mannerism.

I was so overwhelmed by his flashiness that I nicknamed him Uncle Blaster. I have spent some truly great moments in his company. Many interesting events, both comical and adventurous, that I cherish in my memory, have occurred with him. One such event I have also recorded in this book.

I was so charmed by the booming glamour of so-called crop protection hunting that most of my activities centered around this sport. I spent my time in an atmosphere of chase. I fail to record a day when I did not either sit on *machans* or in a natural concealment or in a hunter's pit in wait for the game, or a day when I did not listen to the crack of a rifle or the bang of the shotgun, or the raucous yells of beaters and bore a testimony to a variety of trophies being brought into the home. There were two factors that had chiefly enticed me into this past time. The first was my amateurish age in which the craving to do something extraordinary rests in every young heart, and the second was the influence of my elders, especially of Uncle Blaster, who wanted me to take up this sport to carry on the legacy of the family.

Later, with the passage of time, as I attained maturity of thought, I became conscious of the decline of the jungles all around me. The virgin Savannah lands were gradually being encroached upon and cleared of their vegetation. I registered a first hand knowledge of the decline of a number of sizeably fragmented blocks of bush land that had irretrievably disappeared from the scene. The gnawing away of the habitat had consequently affected the plethora of avian and ungulate life. The grass around the water pond had been replaced by maize fields. Human pressure had mounted so much that the migratory birds had stopped sheltering in the old pond of Larti. By the middle of the seventies, when I reached late teenage, the wildlife had already become very thin on the ground. Only a marginal population of the wild boars was eking out its harassed existence and I was pained to realise that even their precarious subsistence of life, was becoming progressively difficult this evident environmental deterioration perplexed my boyish thinking. In my sub-conscious mind I began to wonder about the relevance of the hunter's destruction. This enigma soon became apparent and made me look at things from a comparative angle. I recalled as to how previously, in a single hour's drive through the forest, we used to discover several worthwhile shooting animals and in those days as a rule, we never returned empty-handed without a pot animal for dinner. In a remarkably short time the rampant hunting had denuded the forest so badly that even the long distance beats or long day's assiduous bullock cart rounds could hardly meet with the requirement of a pot hunter. Under such devastated conditions, whenever once in a week or fortnight I gunned down a stray creature, I found myself unable to justify my action. My slaughterous operations only brought me a deep sense of repentence. Gradually, the

discomfort became more and more frequent and made the game of hunting less thrilling for me and soon I started to regard it as repugnant. I had no further desire to gun down any creature although this was contrary to the then prevalent mood of my family. I took a completely different stance. Finally, that very year I bade a permanent farewell to my hunting days but nevertheless I continued to be fascinated by firearms. Once I had learnt to handle them with care, they gave me an enormous pleasure and they still continue to remain a major passion of my life. Although I had abandoned hunting animals altogether, yet my jungle associates continued to remain in my company.

I acknowledge it to be the greatest of my privileges to have grown up in the company of distinguished naturalists, wildlifers and a few splendid native and professional hunters. To my mind they were the most colourful people I have ever associated with up till now in my life. The first one among them is a professional hunter named M. Haider Mamman. He was then an employee of a Delhi-based *shikar* firm called Indian Shikar and Tours Private Limited. This firm is credited to have supervised hunting of three hundred tigers, out of which a hundred and thirty-two tigers were directly shot under the supervision of Mamman Uncle.

The second prominent person in the field of my knowledge was now late Chhotey Pasi of Larti. He was a curious character and his understanding of the jungle secrets was profound to an amazing extent. I gratefully attribute the credit of my knowledge of the jungle to him. He is largely responsible for providing me a substantial foundation in this field. He taught me about the finer distinctive points of the jungle geography, its nature, peculiarities, character and scope. Chhotey was a skilled hunter, but what made him different from other hunters was the quality of his knowledge about animals. He often said that the knowledge of the hunter is generally limited to serving his purpose of killing. Since it comes to him in a conventional way of trailing for a trophy and the art has a relatively restricted scope, a hunter learns only about those idiosyncracies of animals which help him in their destruction. Thus, it gets confined only to those behavioural patterns which come in response to human harassment. But the amount of familiarity an observer cultivates with the animal provides him with greater and more complex information about the animal. It reveals the remote facets of a creature's mind when he freely ventures from his home monitored by the hidden eyes of a chary watcher. Thus, Chhotey was the rare combination of both the aspects of jungle knowledge and this made him unparalleled in his calibre. At the risk of grave personal dangers, he had the boldness to penetrate into the most inaccessible domains of tigers. He had built up a few hide-outs and *machans* in the jungle where he occasionally went to keep a watch on animal movements, with absolutely no intention to harm them.

I often availed the opportunity to accompany him on his long moon night vigils. There, from the *machans* and hide-outs, I learnt a great deal about animals. Though I cannot myself evaluate the extent to which my observations helped me develop an insight into animal behaviour, the impressions assimilated by me in those early times of life have certainly served me a great deal to acquire a vital, latent modicum of discernment in analysing and understanding the surreptitious characteristics of the jungle.

My diaries contain more than a thousand pages of notes in which I have preserved the details of my effrontery I have lived through since my childhood and the adventures performed both casually and committedly. The most romantic pages are those in which I have recorded a few early encounters with the aberrant wild animals in which I was lucky to emerge unscathed. I think that the then impetuous rashness of youth could well have resulted in the supply of my name to the obituary columns of the daily newspapers and that would have been very natural. I systematically learnt how to avoid danger and yet obtain good results in my hobby of recording timeless fixtures of wildlife.

I believe, if wildlife observations are rendered a simple process completely devoid of the element of danger, a majority of naturalists would discover little interest in pursuit of this hobby.

3

Tigers and Wild Dogs

If you travel on the metalled road from Nighasan to Palia, at its thirtieth mile-stone, you would find a dusty road that branches out from it and meanders towards the north. This road winds between agricultural fields for about two furlongs. Amidst the seasonal crops, the fields are largely laden with sugarcane. Winding gradually through marshy terrain, the road finally terminates at a village called Bela Kalan. It is a historic and prosperous settlement. Here the reflection of the dogmatic customs practiced in the past are still obvious. Echos of the heyday of feudalism when the village was owned by the princely rulers of Singahi State still haunt the minds of people. The family is even today revered by the masses. Insubordination to their ancestral masters is out of question, however pluralistic and egalitarian Indian society may have become. A massive *kothi* that stands in the centre of the village was built by Kunwar Dilpat Shah in the first quarter of this century. He was believed to be the best running game shot in the world. From the day of its construction, the *kothi* was utilised as a hunting camp house by the Maharaj Kumar of Vijayanagaram better known as Vizzy among his cricketer fans. He is credited with having shot a record number of four hundred tigers, a majority of them were claimed in the Terai area of Kheri district. The great hunter met his sad end in this region when a tigeress, wounded by him, charged on his elephant. The animal unable to stand the attack bolted throwing Vizzy on the ground. He received serious internal injuries and later succumbed to them.

A grand trail of forest running opposite this gorgeous structure is called Salookapur range which now forms one of the major blocks of the Dudhwa National Park. In addition to the great cats and their prey, this area is also known to be the habitat of packs of wild dogs. They are foes of all living creatures and are particularly destructive to sambhar and cheetal which they follow relentlessly and tear limb from limb while still alive.

The wild dog is the only flesh-eating animal which does not detest his own kind. Whereas a tiger or leopard will send their own species packing by furious demonstrations, the wild dogs are shrewd enough to realise the importance of their numbers. If two separate groups of wild dogs encounter each other, they do not reproach but instead, welcome each other and ultimately unite into a single formidable group. This force of unity makes them the most threatening hunters of the jungle.

Their hunt is one of the most unpleasant events to watch, but still one cannot refrain from appreciating the intelligent methodology employed by them in the act of hunting. The first change occurs upon locating the prey. As the pack decides to follow it, the beasts divide into two discrete groups. Giving weird and high pitched cries, one group gives chase to the quarry. The second group, breaking away in a blanking movement, tries to run ahead of their quarry so as to cover up both flanks of the pursued animal. Wild dogs refrain from violent outburst of speed. There is no undue hurry in their pursuit. They proceed at a steady tireless pace, emitting a series of yells that resembles the whistling cry of birds rather than of a dog. Thus, moving in unison they completely exhaust their prey and ambush it as it dashes past them. The runners on the flanks keep attacking the animal, disemboweling and emasculating it. At times, they will bite off his ears and even try to gouge out its eyes. The poor victim's flight is progressively hindered until both the flanks join to complete the job.

If comprised by a good number, a pack of wild dogs will not think twice about attacking even a leopard or a tiger. Records of natural history carry sufficient evidence of tigers being killed and eaten by wild dogs. Such a fateful encounter does not take place simply because carnivores are included in the prey list of wild dogs, but more because of accidental meetings over a particular kill. Once dogs are determined to charge, the fate of their victims is sealed.

Owing to their notoriety the wild dogs were classified in the category of vermin. During the British Rule in India, an award of ten rupees each was kept on their head. It was a great amount in those days, and this incentive had induced several licensed game hunters to take up their killing, so that the dog population remained under check.

I am told by old inhabitants of the area that once, prior to this wanton elimination, in the decade of the thirties, the red dog population had greatly increased and a few packs had even taken to attack domestic cattle, thereby they had become a serious menace to country side settlement. Finally, the forest authorities were compelled to launch an "operation slaughter". It was taken up by the game scouts and a reasonable number of dogs were exterminated. As their number dwindled, threat to animal life too waned. The persecuted herbivores that had earlier moved out of affected areas, again returned to their favourite habitats. But, before I proceed further in my narrative, I would state from my personal experience that just because of their hideout hunts, the game does not necessarily migrate from the area. I have seen wild dogs in many forests, living in the vicinity of sambhar and spotted-deer herds, who are least jittery of their presence.

Both the aforementioned episodes prove that wild dogs are prolific breeders. Till the sixties their population remained at a steady level, and they could be found in Salookapur, Sonaripur and Bilrayan shooting blocks. But now, for some inexplicable reason, their population has nosedived and rarely does one encounter them in these areas.

In my childhood days, forests of Salookapur were my

favourite spots for loitering, and in them I have had several little adventures that are still memorable because of their unsurpassable variety.

In the winter of 1967, I happened to visit Bela with my grandmother in response to an invitation of a distant relative. By this time, I had learnt enough about the methods of animal tracking, to decipher their calls, to recognise their signs and partially about hunting. In the past years I had visited Bela twice and during my stay, I had raised a large company of friends in this village. So whenever I visited this area, I was naturally promised a good entertainment. But this time on arrival at Bela, my disappointment knew no bounds to learn that the young boys were not allowed to go out on jungle expeditions because an extraordinarily offensive pack of wild dogs had made its abode in the vicinity. It was just two days before, at the outskirts of the village that they had killed a mule belonging to a poor trader and prior to that a few domestic goats. Although dogs have never been known to attack human beings, we were advised to refrain from careless wanderings as long the pack was around. The elders of the family were very firm in their decision, and no amount of debate, argument or reasoning on my part could dilute their conviction. Eventually, feeling quite disheartened in the absence of any opportunity to savour nature's pleasures, and when all looked drab and lacking in liveliness, I had to stay back in the village and spend my time in the most humdrum way. Then one day, an interesting incident occurred and the dogs met their match in a pair of tigers. The consequences of the incident were dreadful, yet advantageous to our interests, as they automatically removed the ban imposed on our outdoor activities. This incident was witnessed by two labourers of Bela, from whom I learnt the whole account in detail.

It so happened that in the close by Salookapur shooting

block, a dusty road which had been badly damaged in the preceding rainy season was being repaired by the Public Works Department.

It was about two miles inside the jungle. The contractor was a local man. So he had employed a number of labourers from surrounding areas. These included two men from Bela, named Jharkhoo and Buddhoo, who were hired to work as charcoal burners. A temporary camp had been erected in the jungle to provide shelter to labourers but these two men preferred not to stay there for the night. Since the village was not far from the road, they regularly went to the work site in the morning and came back to their homes well before dark.

On that particular day, a sudden chill had been brought about by the cold wave, worsening the bite of the winter. The men were inadequately clothed to ward off the cold, which was bound to worsen by the evening. So the men left early and proceeded for the village. They walked one behind the other along the banks of Suheli river. That day they opted to take a shorter route to return home through a thick belt of *nurkul* (reed) grass that spread luxuriously on both sides of the river. At last they reached the point from where they had to cross the river and descended the embankment. There was no bridge across the river but a big Sal tree which had fallen during a raging storm sometime ago, served the purpose of a temporary bridge. As they took the first few delicate steps on this tree bridge, the leading man noticed a pair of tigers just across the river. They were lying on a sandy bluff, enjoying the fading warmth of the sun.

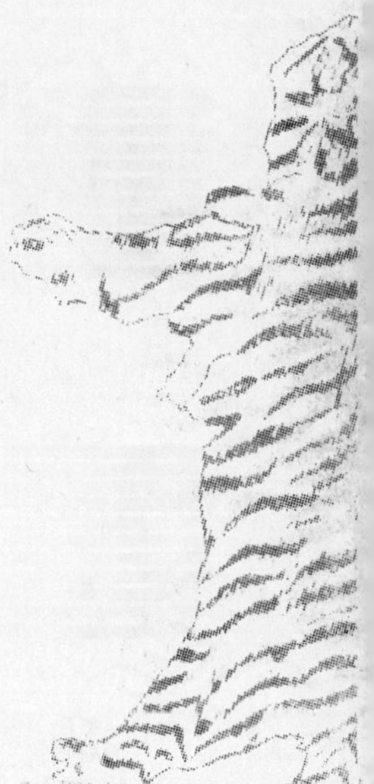

The man halted in their track, it was impossible to cross the bridge as long as the tigers stayed there. The only advisable proposition was to wait until the tigers cleared off from the scene before they could resume their journey. Though the evening was approaching fast and the cold was getting worse, the helpless men first gained their safety on a high perch of a tree and began their long and tiring wait for the tigers to move out and also watch the surroundings. A couple of kingfishers and white herons were flapping down the river. A fish eagle hovering over the water caught a fish with lighting speed in just one move, and landed incredibly close to the men. As she looked at them, she screeched in acute alarm, flapped her wings and sailed hastily across the river. A pair of the hispid hare bounded in and out of the bushes by the riverside, A bizarre community was knit together by the river and its provender.

The men sat there for over an hour, trying to judge the mind of the tigers who seemed in no mood to clear out of the place. The idea of spending a night on the tree was treacherous for the men. Now as the twilight was being succeeded by the advancing darkness, the men sitting on the tree heard sounds of uncertain character, a medley of weird and queer tintinnabulations. The notes were arresting, menacing and provocative, inter-mingled with some sharp and high pitched, shrill, wail-like cries. At first, they could not define its origin but as the sounds came closer, their volume increased they became more clear and then they did not take much time to recognize these intonations. To their horror and prickle of excitement they realized that it was a pack of dogs in the process of chase, to destroy its moribund prey. The sounds indicated that the pack was heading towards the river. As the dogs approached rapidly, the men saw across the river, towards the jungle to their right, a heavy body forcing its way through every obstruction. After a few moments the drumming sounds of the hooves increased and a magnificent cheetal stag galloping madly, exploded out from the tangle of jancus grass and undergrowth. At the sight of the river, he turned and ploughed a wide path for the water as fast as he could.

For, here was ray of hope and it seemed to offer him the last chance of escaping from the murderous pursuit of savage beasts. He looked terribly exhausted probably from the persistent run of a distance longer than which his stamina could normally sustain. Splashes of foam and blood sprayed from his mouth, the deep gashes torn in his neck, shoulder and haunches were conspicuous even from a distance and the blood coursing in red rivers all over his body ran down the flanks from many inflicted wounds. He seemed to take every bound with a prodigious effort. His eyes were terror stricken and bulging out with the expectancy of a ghastly disaster. In his sheer desperation to escape the scourage, he had evidently lost his sense of direction, in darting further he dashed his long symmetrical antlers against the trunk of a silk cotton tree. A sharp clanking sound echoed in the atmosphere, the crash must have hurt him severely, but he quickly regained his footing and again made for the river. Surprisingly, he had remained oblivious of the pair of the resting tigers and it was when he was about to dash in between them that he perceived their presence and suddenly diverted at the last moment in a mancouvre to elude and by-pass them.

The tigers were now excited and they showed a tremendous interest in the prey that had come to them asking to be killed. The male lost no time, he readily stood up, and with a sudden rush launched a lethal attack upon the cheetal. As if thrown by a powerful spring his body temporarily elongated making him land directly on the stag's back, with his fangs and claws buried deep into his tender flesh, the striped body completely covered the stags face and chest. The cheetal fell down on the ground, crushed under the sudden weight of the tiger. He frantically beat his hooves and let out an agonised bellow of terror, his muscles quivered for some brief moments amidst gurgling, choking sounds he lay awaiting his death in patient resignation. His breath ceased to function as soon as the tiger, delivering a mighty blow, broke the bone of its vertibral column.

As the tiger was preparing to drag the kill to his partner, who was now joyfully enthusiastic about it, the pack of wild-dogs brokeout of the same tangle of jancus grass. They looked least startled at the unexpected appearance of tigers, the only thing they did was to stop abruptly and take on an alert guard. They displayed no sign of palpable unease but then

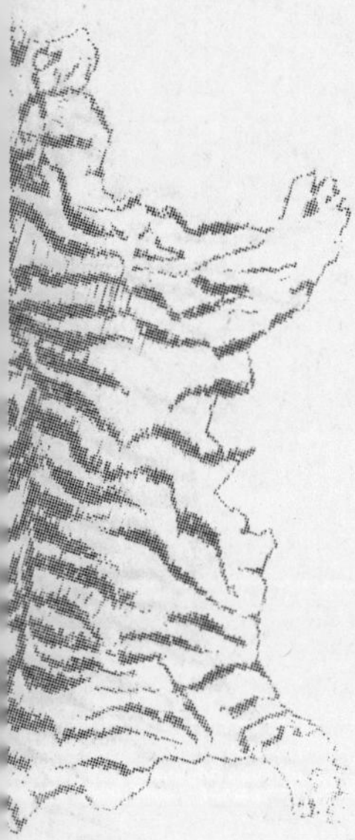

ostensibly the tigers were not ready to take them that casually. At the sight of wild dogs the male tiger dropped the kill on the ground and looked at them. Eyes held eyes, savagely and unflinchingly, a deadly hatred in the entire attitude of both the parties became eminently perceptible. The tiger bared his fangs and letout a series of nerve shattering roars, that seemed to consume all the breath of his lungs. It was apparently intended to terrorize and drive them away, astutely at the same time, the tiger did not forget to keep the cheetal's body secure with his fore-paw. The dogs stayed where they were, and continued their frenzied yelps. The tigress had so far not shown any sign of aggression, rather she had been watching the drama with interest, but seeing the omnious counter-attack of dogs she now decided to act. From her sitting position she began to skulk along, furtively and soundlessly. Her white belly almost swept the ground, her furious eyes were glaring fixedly at the dogs exactly like those of a cat who looks at a bird with utmost intentness. She finally got up and moved intentionally in the direction of the wild dogs. In support of her mate, she also began to emit her violent full throated roars. Soon the majestic challenge of the royal pair reached its zenith of power and the encompassing jungle began to resound like an electrified thunder clap. It was not only a challenge to the dogs but was to all living creatures of the wild.

The horrid sounds were terribly unnerving to the men. Sitting on the tree, they clutched its branches even more firmly to prevent their unceremonious fall. But the dogs on the other hand remained unflinching, they neither advanced, nor retreated, their gory jaws half-open, dripped saliva as they barked a lot of abuse at this unwanted intervention by their rival predatory slayers. All this time and very shrewdly they were rather, trying to estimate the gravity of the situation. The whole jungle had tensed with the sound of the reverberating vibrations of great power being released by the tigers. Time seemed suspended. The earth, trees and the atmosphere quivered with the mighty reverberations, disturbing many wading birds who took to precipitate flights. Even the fruit bats screeched, and flapping their wings heavily, clearedout of the area. Still the dogs remained unruffled and expressionless. They stood their ground and regarded their enemies with vicious intent. There was a noticeable deadly menace in their entire rigid stance. The men counted them, they were twelve in number, exactly a dozen.

The wild dogs strategy is designed in accordance with the circumstance. The most important considerations are the number of attackers and the kind of animal which is being attacked. Their cunning strength, agility, ferocity, bluff, confidence in attack or defence is superb, no man can ever teach them a single trick in the game of life or death. Within seconds the dogs had decided their strategy. The next instance with a lethal discipline that is typical of martial killers, they divided into two groups, six dogs in each group and advanced separately in a determined manner to surround the tiger and the tigress. Their high pitched yelping had now given way to long drawn bays, interspersed with curious metelic sounds. These calls are the urgent invitations to summon up an additional force. They pronounce an important message that every other wild dog within the hearing distance of their cries should rush to help the particular pack which has now set upon some formidable encounter. The experts of animal acoustics often also associate them with sonorous whistling type of nodes. These sounds are those which are always preceded by overwhelming sentiments and a noteworthy discipline of brotherhood.

The male tiger listened to those sounds, his countenance was evidently taken over by a sudden feeling of uneasiness. Doubt, tension, fear and rage flitted across his face, and he scattered the earth with a hard stroke of his fore-paw while his steady eyes never wavered from the malevolent stares of his ancient and trecherous foes. The tigers had grasped the perilous situation, which, with every passing seconds was slipping out of their hands, in favour of their cruel unruffled adversaries.

The whole scene was tremendous, alive with a touch of an elemental violence, infact the stage had already been set for a remarkably spectacular titanic struggle. These were going to be the moments of superb thrill. Virtually the moments for history, a scene that was to become a memory which even the passage of many years would not be able to efface.

Having circled the tigers, the wild dogs started approaching inwards by slowly shortening the circle, the same was done with the tigress. By now both the cats had realized that granting more time to the dogs was rather fool hardy, so with the strength born out of sheer desperation and terror, the tigress intitiated the offensive. Whirling around in a nervous violent state and with almost incredible agility, she swept her extended tallons and slapped wildly to her right and left. This lightening round must have lasted for a couple of seconds, when the attack ceased as abruptly as it had began. She was a predator after all and that too of the highest order, whose basic instinct of survival existed in the game of blood. Obviously, she was profficient in her traits and none could have taught her in the matters of ring tactics. Her foot work was superb and she knew every tactical art and how to use them under the dictates of circumstances. Now as its result, three wild dogs had fallen and one had been sent flying, almost hurled into the air by the terrific impact, dropping with a thud at a distance of almost 15 feet from the main battle arena. However, with amazing rapidity, two of them again stood erect and recovered their poise. Seeing that things were getting hard, the tiger also followed his mate's policies. He drew himself into a ball, his tail lashed the ground with furious blows that raised a lot of dust and extending his fierce paws, he immediately launched a crackdown on the dogs that had recovered and resumed the battle.

Meanwhile, the remaining dogs, forming a fatal co-ordination, once more resolutely launched an attack on the tiger's rear. It was an astute and effective manoeuvre and a desperate and irritated tiger once again turned about to face the vehement attackers. One of them was relentlessly slapped and sent in the background while the rest withdrew and dispersed strategically. Now only seven dogs had remained fit to battle against the mighty predators. Three dogs lay moaning on the ground while two of them had been knocked down for a full count. This outcome emboldened the spirit of the tigers and they once again charged on the dogs with threatening and perceivably triumphant notes issuing from their throats. They extended their tallons and in just two swift boxes bundled off two more dogs, injuring them mortally. Meanwhile, one of the severely crippled, pain-maddened animals tried to escape the propinquity of its tormentors in a limping gait but it soon collapsed on the ground and lay still. Seeing the signs of life remaining in him, the tigress turned, pounced on the miserable creature and embedded her fangs in his stiff flesh. While she was tearing away at the dog's body, all the remaining five dogs attacked her from the back and once again succeeded in tearing out a substantial chunk of flesh from her hind portion.

The men looked at the ghastly drama benumbed and in bewilderment they were still expecting that the reinforcement calls would be answered as there were many wild-dogs in the area. But in the attending moments, probably no member of their tribe was present in the close vicinity, for even after the passage of considerable time not even a single dog had turned up on the site. The entire scene was that of prehistoric primordial wilder days: an extremely rare experience for the humans to have witnessed. As the dogs combated with the mighty predators to death, it was evident that the joint force of the two vastly superior cats was much better equipped to meet their vehement challenge.

By now the harassed members of the pack began to feel the

strain of this disastrous onslaught. They had committed an unpardonable mistake of going for two tigers simultaneously, and now having lost more than half of their pack, they had come to realize that they faced the threat of being wiped out themselves. Any more attempt to fight on their part, could only serve to accentuate the existing degree of suicidal peril. The fight was more or less concluded and suddenly they twisted their tails and within a split second vanished from the scene like a wisp of smoke. The belligerent pair of tigers was in no mood to pardon them so they too went after them, following them into the depths of the jungle. A wild scene of violently swaying grass-stems was seen and soon they were all lost in the thickening darkness.

The men did not dare to come down from their perches, they sat there with no option but to continue an uncomfortable night, shivering in the bitter cold and listening to the feeble cries of badly mutilated dogs, lying thoroughly incapacitated on the bank of the river. The two tigers later returned to the site, when the darkness was intense but for the flimsy glimmer of the twinkling stars that had began to wink down over the stage from the dark canopy of sky overhead. The visibility was far from being good but peering hard through that ethereal miserable light and against the sharply cut out line of Sal forest in the back ground looking dark on the other side of the embankment, the men could make out the dim profiles of tiger and tigress moving here and there. The big cats were still in a vile temper since they attacked the injured dogs and killed them very quickly with a speed matching their fury. Having accomplished this they sat and relaxed for some moments and then commenced to eat the dogs. But their smouldering desire for vengeance had not yet perished. Giving vent to it, they tore up the bodies of the remaining dogs into shreds. The cheetal was simply forgotten and was left untouched, probably because of the knowledge that when one chews the flesh of his detested enemy it makes the best curry. Around mid-night, having gorged enough flesh, the tigers disappeared in the thickets and did not return. An accute silence corresponding to that of a grave settled down on the atmosphere as the drama concluded.

This event is a live example of the reckless bravery of the wild dogs. Despite their exertion and wounds, the determination of these dogs is unbeatable, and had their contingent arrived in due time, the fate of the tigers would certainly have been sealed. The dogs in such cases do not relax until their pursuit has been finally terminated.

At dawn, the men left the forest and hurried nervously into the village. Their story thrilled the natives and several men claimed to have heard the tiger's roaring the previous evening. Now they all were interested to see the remains. Several men armed themselves with all kinds of primitive weapons and immediately left for the scene of the occurrence. Incidentally, that day I was the only boy around in the village who could handle a gun properly. Thus, it came upon me to accompany them, and the elders permitted me to go, as the mob pressure grew on them. In an hour's walk, we reached the spot, and there we found the ghastly evidence of the fight. The grass was all smeared with sticky and thick blood that had turned dark brown under the exposure of the sun. Mutilated remains of dogs, a few of them almost unrecognisable, lay scattered all round. There were bitten off heads, claws and many legs with large pieces of flesh adhering to them. The tigers had eaten some quantity of flesh from every dog's body. Flocks of scraggy-neck vultures were seen soaring in the high heavens busy in their routine work of carefully scanning the earth below for the signs of death. Quite a few of them, who definitely possessed a better eyesight had started to swoop down on the ground but because of the disheartening human presence had not yet settled comfortably on their job.

The mob accompanying me comprised mostly of ardent jungle lovers. They were fairly interested in knowing the details of the encounter. We stayed there till late afternoon, and it gave me an opportunity to discover more and more about the sequence of the occurrence. My time was happily spent in studying the pug marks of the tigers, that were deeply imprinted all over the sandy river embankment. I tried to reconstruct the chain of the story by more tell-tale signs that lay strewn all over the place. And later I was satisfied to find that they were exactly in accordance with the version of eye witnesses of the fight.

4

The Saintly Tiger and Poachers

(I)

Around 16 kms to the south of Palia and 6 kms inside the old Maholi reserve forest adjacent to the Kila Bani Range of Dudhwa Tiger Reserve, lies a small farm known as Grant no. 10. It is a remote and underdeveloped region, abounding in blood-sucking leeches and ticks. In the rainy season their number grows to an enormous multitude and throughout the season they remain a constant source of irritation and trouble to the local populace. They normally thrive on the wild and domestic animals which become literally covered with them specially with the ticks that are over two inches long in size and are generally known as *dans* in Terai. These stick to the delicate portions of their bodies, greedily feeding on their blood and swelling like small bunches of cherries. They also occasionally take to the unguarded human beings, biting all over their bodies in hundreds of places. When a leech sticks to a human body its bite is least painful and usually goes unnoticed for it injects an anti-pain and anti-coagualent which prevents natural clotting of blood and once a leech has taken a substantial meal it can go without further food for over a month. Contrary to this, the ticks engorge themselves with ten times their body weight in blood but they need at least one good meal almost everyday. Their mouth parts are specialised for piercing and they are said to locate the presence of their host by the carbondioxide which it exhales. Tick bites are very painful and often the wounds that

are left last for over a month. The scratching of these wounds may temporarily provide relief but in the process they turn more sour and become maddeningly irritating. For this reason, every year in the rains this area becomes a virtual scene of hell and on the other hand with the approach of winter when the monsoon abates, the landscape acquires an extremely pleasant ambience that is second-to-none in this country.

In the north-east of this Grant a small river called Suheli meanders down its course from Nepal into India travelling through the humid forests over sandbanks and dead logs. It forms a natural boundary of Dudhwa National Park. To the south of it is a belt of grass followed by a great expanse of farm lands and in the north, *jamun* and other wet-land trees stand half submerged in the water. On the escarpment above is the plantation of euclyptus trees interspersed with teak and other hard woods and before the regular Sal forest starts, there lies an eerie land-scape of bare tree trunks and creepers where many animals live in retreat from man.

For miles the course of Suheli is dotted with many big and small farms, all of which are called grants. They are actually the chunks of land that were bestowed by the British to their loyal allies, more precisely the influential men who, during the period of great Indian mutiny had helped in saving the lives of their families from the onslaught of rebels and later also in the restoration of their powers against the uprising. A few of these grants may bear some name but they are better known to the people by their numbers and in local parlance they are called *Girants.* Falling in Terai this area is extremely fertile and enjoys a heavy rain fall and is a site of many plantations producing every conceivable crop but above all sugarcane, being a most profitable venture is significantly most potential crop of Terai. These waving seas largely dominate the fields for almost the whole year.

In the summer of 1978, I had come to the grant in response to a long standing invitation of Thakur P.N. Singh of Maholi. He is meticulous and a social landlord of the area, fond of meeting old friends and so lavishly entertaining them that at times it rather becomes embarrassing. While I was in Lucknow I had learnt through correspondence from him, that for the last two years a tiger had migrated into his farm, from the nearby jungle. At first, he only used to prowl through his farm as his territorial beat covered both the jungle and a substantial part of the agricultural fields then later for many accountable reasons he began to like the open surroundings and that too epecially P.N. Singh's farm. In the course of time he adapted himself so well that he finally preferred to change his home from jungle to fields and now at present he had become a permanent resident in a particular cane belt falling around the only tubewell of the area. The tiger's fondness for the cane habitat and a round-the-clock availability of water due to the close by tubewell, had made his movements confined to a restricted area making him more or less a localised predator.

Although he had been here for over two years none of the villagers had shared any unpleasant experience about him. The tiger seemed quite unconcerned with the rest of the world and was more shy and reserved in his activities than his fellow beings. During those years of stay in human proximity he had displayed a few unusual gestures that seemed unlikely to his tribe's character and with them many stories pertaining to his goodness had become prevalent in the surrounding areas.

One most popular amongst them was quoted as an exceptional example of his maturity and tranquility. It so happened that on one fine morning of the winter season when the sun was shining with all its warmth a woman labourer laid her eight month old child on a mat near a Mahua tree and herself went to work in the wheat field. While ploughing its furrows she strayed away for over 100 mts. from her child but not forgetting to keep an eye on him when she looked up from there

she found him sitting happily and playing with a few dry twigs that had fallen down the Mahua tree. Right at that very moment, a huge tiger emerged from behind the tree. Its black and yellow stripes gleamed resplendently in the bright light of day. He stood, as measured later, just seven meters behind the child and surveyed the country from there. The child was engrossed in his play. He had no idea of a fierce predator standing behind him, but the mother was horrified at this sight of the unexpected emergence of the beast. Her shock was so intense that like a statue she stood rooted to the spot and no voice came out of her chalked throat. She watched her child in a completely helpless state but the tiger remained gentle in his behaviour. He just gave a casual glance at the unguarded child, stood there for around half a minute as if to say, "Hallo Baby, where is your mother? You are too small to stay alone." He turned and casually walked back into the grass from which he had recently emerged.

The mother could not believe her eyes, and frantically ran and picked up her child, showering her love in hugs and kisses. She wondered about the noble tiger who had spared the life of her child who was completely at his mercy. Later, when she narrated this incident to the local people she was told that this tiger was too good to be believed. He had already established a reputation for his good nature and in this event he had shown his extraordinary kind gesture. The men appreciated it aloud and from that very day many villagers fondly gave him a name of *Santji* meaning a saint who is harmless and accommodating to the world, at times at personal cost.

Every year at the inception of the cane felling season that starts from mid November till the end of May, the farm tigers are known to be a great nuisance. Harvesting of a tiger occupied cane crop is an extremely difficult affair. Labourers are not ready to risk their lives in such fields and even if somehow, they are induced to work on a high payment they encounter many a naughty tiger who as a rule put forth a strong resistance against this act, apparently resenting the erosion of their habitat. In this process several labourers are inevitably mauled or at times even killed by the aggressive tigers, as the felling goes. Numerous incidents regarding the tiger's resistance to human strategy to counter them become daily conversation among the local people.

But this particular tiger was quite different. As if true to his pet name *Sant*, he was never known to stand in the labourer's way. As soon as harvesting would commence he would silently migrate into another patch of crop and in case there was no crop left he would retreat to the tall grass and bushes which fringed the banks of the river and then into the close by jungle. He would then live there till the newly sawed crop had attained enough height to provide him with nominally sufficient concealment. Then, he invariably returned to his favourite habitat.

The tigers had often roared in this area, this was to be expected as the surrounding forest blocks were full of tigers. There were a few other scattered tigers eking out their niggardly existence at the cane fields. They had roared at times and communicated with each other at great length. But from the locality which this tiger was known to inhabit, nobody had ever heard a roar or even a casual moaning. For this reason the villagers believed that there was something wrong with his vocal chords, since, he appeared to be a dumb tiger. The only default on his part which was a necessity for him in the absence of customary prey was his occasional indulgence in cattle killing. At times this loss of cattle was also partially compensated by the tiger's good feline manners.

Owing to the close proximity of the jungle and with no natural or artificial barrier in between, the crops of the villagers were exposed to the depredation of the jungle marauders. At nightfall herds of cheetal, hog deer, sambhar and wild boars always came out to munch the crops, but the tiger's continuous presence in the area kept them discouraged from entering the fields. The crops suffered little damage, so with this solid benefit on their side the villagers around this farm hardly ever cared to guard their own crops in the night. They slept peacefully in the nights, as the tiger was considered a self-appointed and ibeal unpaid watchman. In addition to this protection extended to the crop, the tiger also happened to be a good source of meat supply for a few enterprising men who were not averse to stealing the kill which the tiger procured from the neighbouring jungle or the cropped field.

I decided that this was a right opportunity offered to me to watch this tiger, record some of his habits and capture few of his elegant moves in my camera.

Having duly arrived in Maholi, I stayed at Thakur P.N. Singh's house where I was overwhelmed by my host's courtesy. A big room had been specially kept ready for my stay, loaded with many unnecessary things intended for my comfort. A few buckets of cold water were ready inside the Thakur's house. As I went into the bathroom, a boy servant followed me with a soap and towel in his hand, he was instructed to take off my clothes and bathe me thoroughly himself. I had never been accustomed to this kind of hospitality, so I coolly turned him out and locked the door. Later, I was served with a huge dish of mutton curry and was almost persuaded to eat it all. I knew I needed to eat well, for the Thakur is rather a sensitively susceptible person and his feelings would be greatly offended if I do not duly appreciate his courtesy.

When the feast was over, Thakur along with a team of his servants guided me to the countryside and showed me the expanse of fields where the tiger presently lived and operated. There were many interconnected blocks of sugarcane dotting the area as I saw the dense sea of interlocked crops. I could easily realize the difficulties I would have to face in my attempt to locate my prey in them. The task seemed to require a fair amount of labour as the tiger might be resting at any point anywhere and in any one of them.

Next day, I got up early and set upon the business of his search. Things soon proved up to my expectations as from that day onwards for over a week. I assiduously tried to locate him but I could not succeed in doing so though several times while traversing in the fields I came across his footprints, both old and new that showed the unmistakable course he had taken in his nocturnal depredation. One morning I came across his squirt-like scent mark on the bark of a semal tree. It looked like a pale yellow liquid, its strong pungent smell indicated that only a few hours back it was ejected sub-caudally in a fine jet on the tree, the moist patch was marked approximately at the height of three feet from the ground. Twice I chanced upon his fresh excreta, both the times he had defecated on the scrap mark made by his feet. The tough material such as animal hair, pigments of bones and scales that had passed out unaffected from his digestive system were clearly visible on the outer layer of his droppings. All these times, by sheer misfortune, I always failed to match my timings with his timings of venture and kept missing him all the times.

The days passed and now it was almost a week since I had began to search for the tiger while he inadvertently happened to maintain a safe distance from me. Eventually, one day I felt deeply disappointed by this tiring business as my perambulations had hardly brought forth any results so I thought of abandoning his trail for good. I still had a week's holidays at my disposal, I decided to proceed for Larti at Mailani and spend the rest of my vacations in the company of my old gang namely Chhotey and his accomplices. At that time I had absolutely no idea that while I was thinking on these lines towards evening of that very day the sluggish spell would be suddenly broken with the occurrance of an interesting incident that began with an unintentional act on my part accomplished just out of human sentiment. It later landed me in trouble with some local bad characters and finally as the things went far enough they forced me to take a temporary leave from the area and also of my pursuits. Later, it paved the way for many other incidents that continued to occur at intervals with me for almost over a year. Now I narrate the account. It happened thus.

At a short distance from Thakur's grant nearing the border of the jungle there is a village known by the name of Dharmapur, the inhabitants of this settlement are generally wretched. They work as daily labour in the neighbouring farms while at home their woman folk weave baskets and create other miscellaneous items from the forest products to be sold and bartered for household items at the periodical village market. Besides these two evident occupations, these people are also notorious poachers. This trade is clandestinely practiced by almost all men and women of the village who were, and possibly still are contributing their efforts in making the forests devoid of practically all forms of life.

It was the tenth day of my stay at the grant when I happened to discover this seamier side of their business, at first, I took it casually thinking that like many other natives, the men possibly often killed the animals only to eat, but later as I conversed with the few labourers of Dharmapur who worked at Thakur's farm, overheard their talks and watched their behaviour, I grew suspicious about their affairs. After my initial doubts were confirmed from various sources, I was astonished to learn that here poaching was being regularly practiced by a highly organised group of men who killed deer and other animals and sold their antlers and flesh in the various markets. They had seriously adopted this furtive business as a great source of money as well as a promising career.

On that occasion, although with very little hopes in my

heart I had once again gone out on a stroll over the trail of the elusive tiger, when my attention was attracted by a medley of squeaking sounds. I stopped in my tracks: they were unmistakably coming from the wild boars who appeared to be in a disgruntled mood. I knew at this time of the year, when the spring season was drawing to its close, numerous sounders of wild boars inevitable come out of the jungle and roam about freely in the fields. They munch and destroy the ripe crops on a large scale in the night.

It appeared from the sounds as if two wild boars were in a vile temper and were in a fight with each other. I got curious to catch a glimpse of these animals, so I hastily left the tiger's trail and headed for the field from where the sounds were emanating. Walking cautiously as I neared the particular patch of ripened wheat crop, my eyes happened to detect a movement as I looked intently. I found a thick rope was carefully tied on a big wooden stump, that was fixed deep in the ground, the rope was long and from this point it had run along the ground, inside the wheat field. I stood at one end of the rope and noticed that at short intervals, it shook violently for a couple of moments then slackened down abruptly. It appeared as if some animal, entangled in the rope was trying to extricate itself.

I had known of this device since my childhood. It was a *khaber* or poacher's net, popularly used in Terai area to catch the animals. Following the rope, I entered into the crop and there in the centre of the field I discovered the net stretching elongated on the flattened wheat crops, it was jumping and bouncing with life. Two maddened wild boars were firmly caught inside it, they appeared to have been trying hard for a long time to beat down the obstacle but in this process their snouts, hoofs and tusks had become more firmly entangled in the knotty nettings, making their escape almost an impossible task. I guessed it to be the work of none else than Dharmapur poachers and later I was also proved right in my surmise. I decided to set the animals free, but by now the rope knots had turned too difficult to be disentangled so in order to cut them free I fired two shots, one each at two supporting ropes. The wild boars who had frozen still on the spot on seeing the human presence so close to them now on hearing the report of gun shot resumed their frantic struggle of freedom and within minutes as the ropes had loosened they disentangled themselves, sprang out of the net and raising dust from their hooves bounded away with all their might into a distant gram field.

While I was setting the boars free I was absolutely oblivious of the watchful eyes of the trap setters who were intently noticing my activities from somewhere. My act was uncompromising for all intents and purposes and it was certain to disappoint them, but however angry they might have felt the disheartening sight of gun in my hands prevented them from taking an immediate action against me.

This incident had spurred my interest. I felt motivated to investigate further in this context. I closely inspected the nettings that were used to trap the wild ungulates and found them of high quality. They were even strong enough to catch and hold a tiger. Thick plastic coils of finer variety had been used to prepare them indicating the crime was being committed in an organised manner. It could not be a food catch operation and there was certainly some gang working behind it. I postponed my visit to Mailani and decided to set upon task of finding the culprits.

In the course of time, I made a lot of inquiries in this regard but they hardly elicited any important information. The only fact which surfaced from all the quarters was that some men of Dharmapur were involved in this practice. Meanwhile, the criminals also happened to get the air of it. When they learnt of my efforts they felt offended and wondered why I was doing all this. When nobody, including the forest officials had ever taken so much interest in their activities then why was I poking my nose. They formed their own conclusions about my intentions. I had never known, seen or met these men and had absolutely no desire to harm them. I only wanted to have a good dialogue with them, thinking that would enable me to read their minds and I may somehow be able to educate them about the eco-system and the diminishing wildlife of the area. I wanted to convince them with my view-point and if possible change their mind and attitudes towards their environment.

I had been looking forward to meeting with some of these men. Under a strong misconception of being brought into a systematic trap they thoughtfully decided to teach me a lesson at the earliest, which was later proved by the following incidents.

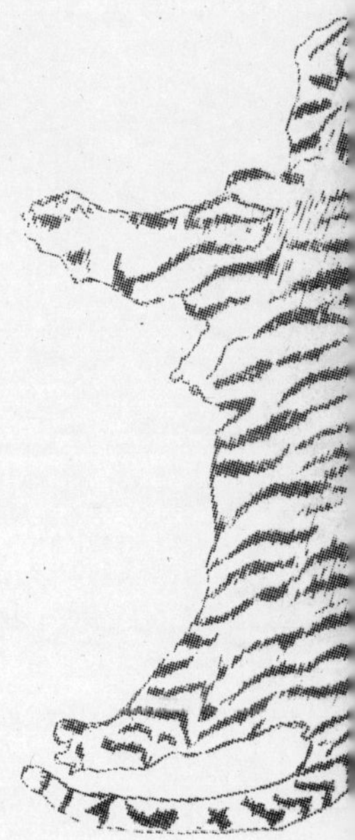

A few days after this event I had to go to the closeby township of Bahmanpur to buy some provisions. It was not a jungle drive so I had not cared to take my gun this time. As I started the motor bike, an old servant of Thakur by the name of Roshan came out of the house and showed his willingness to accompany me. I readily agreed thinking it would be better to have a companion for the way. As the things turned out later his presence made all the difference in the world for me for if he had not accompanied me, this trip would in all probabilit have ended disastrously. For, unknown to me the Dharmapur poachers had kept a track on my movements and on that day, the poachers decided to settle their scores with me.

Once having known that I was unarmed, they went ahead and concealed themselves and waited for me to pass on the road. As my motorcycle negotiated a turn, they suddenly jumped out of the grass which fringed the road and caught me unawares. At first I could not understand and, I mistook them for local bandits but they seemed hardly interested in looting any of my belongings. I was thinking of how to deal with them when one of them spoke truculently in a harsh tone, "Listen, you fool, don't attempt to run or cry out or else you will be killed". They relieved me of my motor cycle and pulled me

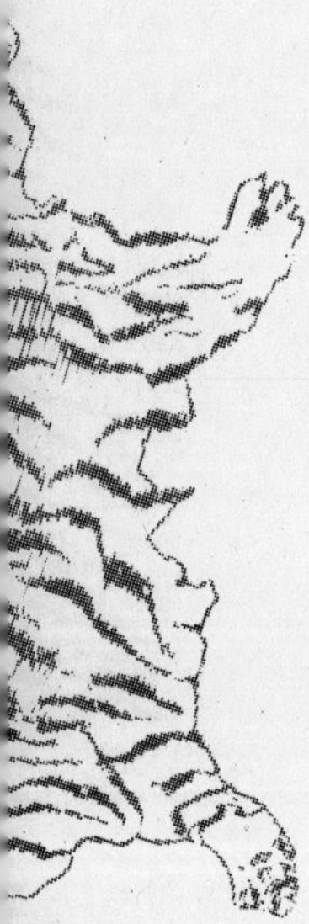

under the shade of acacia tree. Almost simultaneously all of them showered a volley of questions on me, "Tell us you city fly, what person you are working for and why did you release our *shikar*"?

This sentence instantly made me understand their identity. They were the poachers I had been hankering to meet for about a week. I counted, at a glance, eight men, all of whom had covered their faces with the tightly tied scarfres. The only visible part of their face were their eyes, one of the goons had a tremendous height and an equally proportionate physique. His very sight was so terrorising that it made my heart beat in my mouth. Now as there was no escape from the situation, I tried to keep my nerves steady and talked to them politely in a firm voice. They had actually planned to give me a serious bashing, but my steadfast way of talking kept them undecided about their moves. By a stroke of fortune, Roshan happened to recognize one of the goons and this came as a blessing at the most crucial moment. Nevertheless the criminals were resolute in intimidating me. Roshan apologised on my part and tried to pacify and placate them yet they caught hold of my collar and amidst abuses displayed their country made pistols daggers and *kattas* etc., apparently to terrorize and threaten me with dire consequences.The proposition was odd and I with a feeble servant was no match for them, so I had to endure their blows. I was strictly warned that never in future should I attempt to be smart with them. Next time if I did not heed their admonitions, would be thoroughly beaten up, finally with this threat the men punctured my bike with daggers, left me and entered the surrounding grass to vanish from the scene.

This notice given to me was no doubt serious. It instantly put me on guard. It seemed things were not going to be simple at all. I should either give up my efforts to curtail poaching or else I do it with a very strong backing, otherwise the complications were sure to land me in a mess with the poachers. Under the present conditions since I was exposed to very severe physical harm, it was inadvisable for me to stay at the grant. I knew well about Thakur P. N. Singh's limitations. He was influential though he wielded very little ascendancy to counter the threat of this kind of professionally hardened criminals. On the other hand, I also knew about the working of police.

So after much thought and feeling, utterly helpless to challenge the poachers with my meagre resources I finally decided to seek help from Uncle Blaster of Larti. I returned home loosing my temper over punctures and pushing the bike along recklessly and bitterly on the rims. By the time I reached home the tyre and tube had completely blasted out. The same afternoon I packed my belongings and immediately proceeded for Mailani by a local bus. The late evening found me having arrived at my ancestral village where I met my uncle, sitting amidst a dozen barking hounds, feeding them with raw chunks of buffalo meat. I told him the purpose of my visit and briefed him about the happenings of the day, this uncle of mine as I have already mentioned is a typical village feudal. Even today in the days of populist policies, he commands a substantial hold in his area besides being infamous as an influential land shark.

He showed concern at my distress and after hearing me he took my problem seriously. I was happy to see that in the process of narration and without much analysis Uncle Blaster was obliged to make this offence his foremost prestigious issue. As I continued my tale, he became convinced of it being an unbearable disgrace to his great stature. How could anyone dare to challenge his nephew in the district and still worse, threaten his life? By the time my story ended he had already worked himself into a rage, declaring in his growling tone that he would break the bones and take out the entrails of the persons who had dared to set eyes upon me.

Evaluating the situation once again, he decided to act in his own way. The area of Maholi, where I wanted him to help me, was at a distance of 50 kms from Mailani by road. It did not directly fall in the zone of his influence but still he zealously bore the responsibility of dealing with my enemies. Darkness had fallen and as nothing could be done at night I stayed at Larti. Lying in a wooden thatched structure outside the house and feeling an intense buzz of insects, I listened to the old familiar sounds of the jungle all around me and recalled many days and nights I had spent in the recess of these woods. The breeze was deliciously cool, myriads of stars twinkled in the sky. Relaxed in my mind and enjoying that nostalgic atmosphere I fell asleep under the open vault of heaven.

With the coming of dawn the next day, all the ruffians of the area were summoned in the court of 'Uncle Blaster'. In the meantime a local transporter's truck was also requisitioned. Soon an army of men, under the command of one of the trusted toughs, was raised to proceed towards Dharmapur. A tough lesson was to be taught to the villagers. The men assembled in the court had come with all kinds of weapons, their guns, country made pistols, dagger spears, bows, arrows and thick staves etc. presented a truly formidable sight. A few uninvited but enthusiastic volunteers had also arrived with their dogs. I marvelled at the great variety of breeds. A more miserable, mangy, underfed, curly-tailed collection of mongrels would have been difficult to put together. There were cross-breeds of every kind, size and colour. There were dogs as big as an ass and as small as a little cat. The men showed their enthusiasm to participate in the drama and owing to their free of cost availability, they too were readily incorporated in the team.

We all climbed into the truck. Some of the dogs had never been in a truck before. With the sputter of the engine, they became restless and struggled madly to free themselves of their masters, who tried to hold on to them by their tails, legs and necks. A few dogs were more determined strugglers. They worked themselves loose and jumped frantically out of the truck. At quite a few places, we had to stop the vehicle while the dog's owners went chasing after them, caught them and forcibly brought them back.

Eventually after a noisy journey, we reached Dharmapur. Once there, the ruffians began a most formidable display of terror. All inhabitants were unceremoniously asked to gather in the centre of the village. An ominous atmosphere of trepidation was built up. A few of them began sharpening their knives with a flourish in front of the collected villagers, while all of them banged their sticks on the ground, producing a terrorising sound plus raising a lot of dust. All of them also kept raising a cacophony of shouts and abuses directed at the helpless villagers. The more enterprising among the hooligans also fired shots in the air. They also caught and slapped a few idiotic looking persons, who were not supposed to object to this performance. At times, the racket kicked up by the boisterous dogs almost matched the ear-shattering exhortations by the raiding party. But while men kept their distance out of some basic constraints of law the dogs had their free for all, and compensated for the slackness in the proceedings. The army of dogs accompanying the hooligans was no less excited, and it provided them with solid support and kept the village mongrels at bay.

All this action of course was a high voltage drama enacted to impress the inhabitants without mincing words. I was delighted to notice that the show had been a great success. The village chief apologised in a sheepish manner and assumed the immediate responsibility for my safety wherever and whenever I ventured in his area. The culprits were also recognised and the toughs wished to brush-up their martial arts on them. I stopped them from doing so, and after a nominal manhandling, if there is such a thing, the matter was dropped. The style in which the dose was administered had been more effective and up to my satisfaction than the dose itself.

Now that I was safe under the protection of my uncle, I decided to explore and expose the surreptitious activities of Dharmapur villagers and get them punished. I posted complaints to the district and forest officials but none cared for them as they were probably lost in the bureaucratic maze. I came back to Lucknow, where I prepared fresh reports of poaching and sent them to newspapers in Lucknow and Delhi, but nobody bothered to publish them. Then one day, Mr. Y.C. Rai, a senior officer of the Indian Forest Service (IFS) happened to pay me a visit. I explained to him the matter in detail and he took it seriously, and offered to cooperate. But as general probing was not likely to produce the desired results, he advised me to keep a track on poachers and try to collect some evidence against them if possible, as that would strengthen the hands of law. Meanwhile, he assured me that his men would make it a point to take care of suspected villagers. I do not know whether he acted as seriously as he had spoken but through my informed sources of the area the reports of unabated poaching of Dharmapur men kept pouring. Rather in than giving up all hopes, I finally began my own efforts to curtail it.

I organised an anti-poaching squad comprising of a few local people, my old friend. Dr. P. K. Singh of Nighasan willingly assumed the responsibility of its supervision whereas Rajesh Gupta, Krishna Kumar and Sardar Ram Singh and Deep Shah of Singahi took the lead in their areas. My men spent a very tough time in trying to curtail these nefarious activities and in this process they made a lot of enemies among the local populace. The squad probed into several new sad incidents and prepared a list of poachers from many villages namely Tanda, Maholi, Salimabad and other areas, and the list was submitted to the forest department. I do not know what happened to that list later and what kind of actions were taken but all I know is that the poaching activities continued almost as before.

Why I could not do so well was indeed, because of the fact that I was a visitor from Lucknow and not a local man. I came here always with a restricted time at my disposal and due to my misconceptions I awaited help from the boorish enforcement machinery of the government that seemed to need constant motivation to do any work. With this kind of setup I did not expect to succeed easily in my mission. Then one day another poaching incident occurred. It completely disillusioned me and exposed the futility of my efforts made so far in this direction. The event was yet another incarnation of tragedies that are the bane of human and wildlife interactions.

(II)

It was the month of March, and Holi, the festival of colours was drawing near, when, the son of the local priest whose name was Ramu visited his village to spend a week's holiday with his family. He was employed as a guard in a bank and was allotted a DBBL 12 bore gun with a belt of cartridges, which he brought along on his vacation. While he stayed in the village his friends insisted on making a programme for some shooting. In the past days of his boyhood Ramu had indulged in some poaching over waterholes and salt licks. He had a reasonable experience of hunting. This time, he agreed to try his weapon against a few forms of jungle life.

The programme was immediately made. His father came up with a torch loaded with feeble batteries, and both father and son left for a waterhole that lay at a distance of two kilometres to the north of the village. They reached a pithole constructed by poachers in the proximity of the pond exclusively for the purpose of sitting concealed and firing shots at the animals. There the poachers occupied a convenient position inside the hole and to conceal the top of their heads that projected slightly above the ground, they sought shelter behind a few bushes. The pit was located at an ideal spot, just immediately behind it was a thick cluster of bamboo and its front was all open for about 25 yards where it was bordered by the forest from three directions, so from this position poachers commanded a view of the entire water pond.

It was a peaceful day. The sun was just about to set, the red ball of fire was casting its reflection across the sky where it had painted the clouds in the most beautiful colours, they changed from crimson to orange and then into an immaculate purple as the pale celestial disc dropped lower in to the horizon, finally disappearing from the view.

The ground around the pond was deeply ploughed by numerous tracks of lesser game. The signs showed that a large number of animals like sambhar, swamp deer, cheetal, hog deer, *kakkar* and wild boars etc. regularly visited this pond and knowledgeable of this feature, the two men sat contentedly at the pitholes listening to the chorus of night hunting birds that had now come out of their shelters and were enliving the atmosphere with their raucous cries. They were soon followed by the inauspicious howling of jackals. The hungry scavengers seemed to communicate with each other for some information of food. In this atmosphere, the poachers waited for a little more deepening of the dusk that would herald the arrival of animals on the pond.

The light faded fast in the manner of all tropical countries. Darkness has just started to envelop the jungle, when Ramu saw a flock of crimson-headed parrots rising abruptly from the branches of a close by Mahua tree. What had roused them from their roosting place? Why did the parrots do that? He was wondering, when suddenly he became aware of a muffled tread in the grass, that grew across the pond straight in front of him. Here in the middle of the grass patch a leafless teak tree was standing. As it happens, the dry leaves of teak spreading on the ground provide an ideal medium to warn the watcher or hunter about the approach of jungle folk who happens to tread upon them. They make murmuring and crackling sounds even at a very light tread of a jungle cock and if one happens to possess an acute sense of hearing he would surely pick-up even these minor sounds. In the case of big animals, they start rustling and crackling noisily a long time before the intruder comes into sight. Contrary to this phenomena the dry leaves of tamarind tree are soft and in the autumn season when they fall on the ground they form a silky carpet, creating absolutely no sounds when trodden upon. The beasts of prey prefer such type of grounds and when stalking or crouching for a hunt they instinctively choose such strategic area, for it always increases the possibilities of a successful ambush.

Now coming back to my story, on hearing that almost deafening sound Ramu thought that it was some animal, probably much more cautious than normal was coming to quench his thirst. The animals generally do not regard water sites as inviolables where they might drink in peace. They are rightly suspicious and they approach the waterholes with infinite caution. Ramu gestured to his father to lean forward and try to scan the bush to know the identity of the animal. The old man strained his eyes for sometime but he heard no sound nor could he register any eye catching movement. Finally, he took it as Ramu's illusion and telling him to sit relaxed he reverted back to his own position but the sounds that had emanated from within the grass, heard by Ramu had unmistakably betrayed the presence of an animal resting in it. What was he doing there? Ramu thought, not caring for the opinion of his father he wondered why it had not come out? Was he trying to make sure that there was no predator near the pond or had he already sensed the presence of human beings and feeling threatened, had decided to move away to some other distant pond? Ramu kept waiting, a tense time of over ten minutes dragged in acute suspense since the light conditions were also worsening fast. Sufficient darkness had already set in and it had paved way for a temporary but crucial period of uncertainity when the eye sight is very easily deceived by the formation of the different patterns on the ground. At this time of the day the innocent shrubs and bushes assume the menacing appearance of crouching and watching wild beasts. Ramu again gestured to his father to light the torch and wave it over the bush. He was getting too impatient to see the occupant of bush and wanted to end the stalemate.

The gadget which they had brought along was small. It contained a pair of run down batteries, yet as the old man switched it on, a feeble beam of light cut forth in the darkness and lit a pair of emerald eyes lurking a few yard inside the sparse grass on the other end of the pool. Not caring to ascertain the identity of their owner Ramu quickly aimed between the eyes and fired at the animal which did not move even a fraction an inch and collapsed instantaneously almost without a whimper.

The shot, by chance had proved extraordinarily perfect. Ramu was contented with his bag, for a pot animal had been procured and its meat he expected would be sufficient for his friends. He wished to call it a day but his father who had come out on a hunting expedition after a long gap of time was in no mood to leave the pit. In his egregious lust for meat he insisted his son sit silently and wait for more animals who would sooner or later oblige them with their presence. It was natural for the father to think that once or rarely twice in a year his son visited the village and only then he ever got the opportunity to throw a sumptous treat to oblige his community so what was wrong in trying to bag a few more additional animals? Eventually, the old man prevailed over Ramu and made him abandon the idea of quitting the pit. Ramu prepared himself for a long vigil and in compliance with the mood of his father, worked himself up in a butcher's state of mind. He became determined to collect a fair number of animals not only for his friends but for whole of the village assembly.

It was a moonless night, the sky was clear and for some reason the stars were shining more brightly today. They gave enough light to make the ground more visible. Then suddenly the atmosphere changed and heavy clouds began to scuttle across the sky, and within no time the stars were completely obscured and the darkness intensified. A sudden variation in the environment made conditions uncongenial for hunting but the poachers stayed on in the pit, though the darkness severely restricted their vision yet they waited for the animals, relying solely on their sense of hearing.

The minutes dragged on. Some time later Ramu heard the rustle of leaves in the jungle and within no time almost unhesitatingly a small herd of five cheetals broke the cover and appeared in the open. Ramu's father again lit the torch and several pairs of eyes reflected the light. Once more a shot rang in the air and an animal dropped to its note, while the rest of the herd took to a precipitate flight, completely vanishing in the blackness of night. Ramu had still not quenched his thirst for blood. He kept waiting, again at 11 p.m., a lonely sambhar came upon the waterhole. One more bang resonated in the atmosphere and one more casualty was enlisted. Then for the rest of the night the drama continued a spell of doom pervaded over the pond and the heavy thirst of L G Alphamax cartridges took a fair toll of wildlife. All the animals that had been fired upon from the close range precisely less than 20 yds, were never allowed to flinch against the deadly accurate lead balls. Ramu too swelled with pride. This prolonged shooting of the night was no doubt an event to be recorded in the annals of the village history and it was enough to credit him with a rare distinction of being the best-ever hunter of the area.

Ramu did not have to wait long before the sky became flecked with dullish grey lights. Soon, many faint streaks of pink, blue and yellow showed here and there on the eastern horizon. As the light strengthened and the mist thinned down, another unfortunate a colony of peacocks emerged out of the bushes. A couple of males walked majestically to the water with their dowdy females following them in the rear.

Ramu greeted the good morning by shooting a pair of peacock and then with those last kills the butcherous vigil finally came to an end. The poachers came out of the pit, feeling still untired. By the success they lit a *bidi* each and entered the bushes near the pond in order to inspect the extraordinary score of the night; a cheetal here and a cheetal there showed what a noble marksman Ramu had been. The father felt gratified with exultation and singing laurels for him he proceeded to the teak tree to peep into its patch of grass beneath it, particularly to discover the very animal Ramu had first gunned down at the start of the shoot. He entered the grass and as he looked into it a cold chill ran down his spine, his voice chocked and his eyes widened with fear for there was no dead animal but instead a massive tiger, belly to the ground was creeping stealthly upon the unsuspecting man as their eyes met the tiger stopped in his track's. The man was thoroughly intimidated. He screeched a warning, jumped to his feet and ran out of the grass hysterically shouting, *"Sher hai"*, *"Sher hai"* (a tiger is here, a tiger is here) the terrible screams were heard by Ramu. He was taken aback at this information as he had no previous experience of dealing with the carnivores and moreover by now his stock of heavy cartridges was already exhausted in the course of night shooting. He had only a couple of bird shots left in his bag. He did not dare to venture anywhere near the grass. The news rather put him on a night and selfishly concerned with his own safety, he hastily scampered up a tree where his father too was very quick to follow him.

The poachers sat there at the safe perch and having regained their breath, they wondered about the unexpected arrival of the tiger, after much discussion they finally agreed that the tiger had smelt the carcasses of the shot animals lying around the pond and had now come to make a meal of them.

It is not uncommon for a tiger and leopard to take up the job of scavengers. At times they may not deliberately search for signs of death, yet in case of a rightful opportunity they do not seem to deny their privilege. I have known of a few cases in which the dead cattle thrown away by the villagers were heartily devoured by tigers. Recently in one case at Sampurna Nagar, it happened near a farm house where the fetid smell rising from the decomposed buffalo corpse attracted a pair of mating tigers. They duly arrived and amidst the human voices stayed in the area for three days to finish it off at leisure.

The father and son knew about this habit of tigers so stayed on the tree for over an hour and from there they kept looking slyly around all the time but failed to perceive any movement of the tiger. Finally when no tiger came out and they felt confident of being safe, very cautiously they came down the tree and made a run for the village with an idea to fetch a crowd that would help them drive away the formidable creature.

There in Dharmapur for the entire night the villagers had heard the reports of shooting, they were getting impatient to know the results. As they heard the poachers calling loudly in excitement they grasped the situation as though something was grossly wrong. Very soon several men armed with whatever they had assembled to help their friends and within no time a crowd was seen marching for the shooting spot. On having reached there, Ramu signaled his party to halt and

pointed at the teak tree under the shade of which the tiger had concealed himself in a bush. The men quickly set upon their task, drums, tin cans, utensils and other miscellaneous objects were beaten. All men shouted at the top of their voice, the cacophony continued for over five minutes and then feeling spent and exhausted the mob abruptly fell quiet to relax. It was naturally concluded that by now the tiger must have fled away from there. To confirm this surmise, a group of some courageous men closed circumspectly upon the grass patch but there they got the shock of their lives when they found the big cat was still sitting crouched in the grass, looking unflinchingly at them. In anticipation of an attack the men screamed with fear and cleared out from there as fast as possible.

The sight of the tiger had sent the crowd scattering in all the directions. However after sometime, when all the mean reassemble at a spot, panic seemed to have gripped many of them quite strongly, nobody was willing to undertake this operation. A few mature men were absolutely against the idea of putting the human lives in to trouble just to collect the carcasses of few stages when the tiger continues to stay at the pond. It was better to wait and give sometime to the tiger so that he takes his share and himself moves out. Yet, nevertheless there were some impatient avaricious persons who wanted to retrieve the carcass before they begin to decompose in the burning sun.

The next round of planning was more elaborate, it was decided to make use of some fire arms. Country-made and other muzzle loading guns were to be fired into the bush which the tiger had duly occupied. The act was methodically performed and then again a few men who were impelled by the curiosity to ascertain the tiger's presence, reached the tree and peeped into the grass patch. This time they had approached him from a different direction. There at the edge they noticed his tail lying slightly raised on a platform-like formation of small plants. A few knowledgeable observers also claimed to have seen it twitching this action was said to be an indication of tiger's evil temperament. It meant a charge was certain to follow the men could instantly perceive the tiger was employing all his skill to make his rush on their party a complete surprise. They felt a pricking sensation at the back of their necks, took an about turn and bolted once again but luckily the tiger did not press home his charge probably he had felt nervous because of the unexpected number of humans, or he might well have halted in amazement. Meanwhile, a poor native who was in his hurry to bounce away from the spot stumbled upon a fallen tree and fractured the femur bone of his leg.

Now, for third time and after a considerable gap of time the crowd reassembled near a sugarcane field. Some experienced men reviewed the situation, the injured man was in great pain. He somehow managed to drag himself out into the field where he was noticed by the rest of the congregation which immediately provided him an improvised stretcher and dispatched him to the village and from there to Nighasan government dispensary. Nevertheless the accounts of this man were impressive, he told that while he was approaching the bush every cell of body had already warned him that he was in, great danger, actually the tiger had come out of his hideout and finding him alone had began to creep upon him from behind. The great cats generally snatch their victims that way and so was being manoeuvre by the tiger, "He would have decidedly taken me, had I not been quick enough to disappear from the spot" he boasted.

The day was oppressively dry yet a few occasional breath of winds seemed to relieve the stifling heat of the atmosphere. The sun had risen sufficiently high in the sky and with that the village roads too had become busy with the usual traffic of the day. By this time when a shimmering haze was beating down and seeing a nervous mob congregated near the jungle, every passerby was getting interested. They stopped and enquired about what was going on. It was not possible to keep the

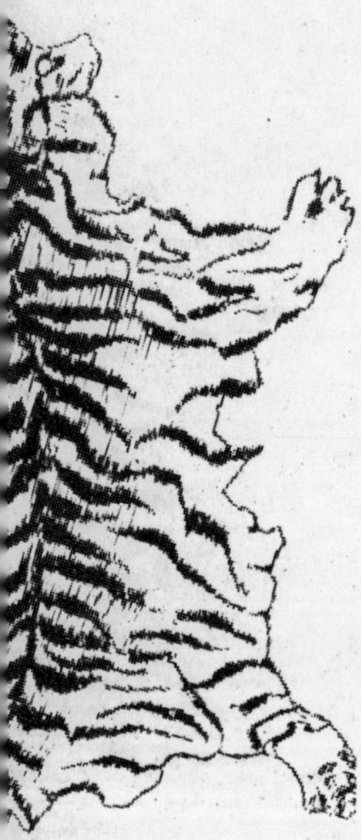

night's escapade a secret. Several cycles and bullock-carts had lined-up on the road near the jungle and their inquisitive owners wanted to find out maximum information about the incident. As more people came to know about the tiger's presence they stopped every now and then to enquire about the latest position. Every detail was of interest and every traveller who heard about the event was happy to carry the news to his own destination.

The hours ticked by, and until afternoon no feasible solution seemed to have emerged. Finally, an intelligent passer-by who for a long-time had been watching this scenario with concern raised a pertinent question whether the tiger had also not been slain in the night's shooting. For the behaviour was something unheard of in the annals of tigers as it was strange for him to remain stationery at a spot for such a long time. Tigers are very intolerant to heat and he should have either taken for the water or should have retired to seek solace in the deeper shades of the jungle. This arid area of intense heat was no place for him to stay on. Then something clicked in the minds of men, the argument was incontrovertable, it seemed to carry the right answer. The group again reached the pond determined to explore the area at any cost. The drama was enacted with courage, and eventually the riddle was solved. The great charging tiger had been dead indeed for a long time. By sheer coincidence his lifeless body had fallen in a position that made him look alive and ready for an ambush rather than being dead. A close examination of his carcass showed he had received the shots from a very close range, a compact bunch of L G Alphamax pellets had pierced him between his eyes. They had spared no time for him to advertise his identity.

Finding the tiger dead, Ramu's morale turned to water though his father who was more cool and practical, immediately set upon the task of eliminating evidences. The carcass of the tiger was quickly removed to some unknown place and buried, there people were so nervous that they did not dare even to collect his skin. The stags too were taken inside the forest where they were quickly dismembered, cleared and distributed, wisdom dictated for Ramu to move out of the district and report on duty with immediate effect. Every weak point was carefully pondered over so that the culprits should not have any difficulty in escaping the clutches of law and the plan was successfully accomplished.

In those days, I had been staying at Nighasan at Mr Sri Prakash Shukla's house and it was after four days that I received the news of the tiger hunt. A local native who sold his goods wandering on a bicycle had carried the information to this town where I happened to hear about it. I offered to pay the informer a handsome *bakshish* if he would agree to guide me to the place where the incident had taken place. This time I was determined to teach a lesson to the inhabitants of Dharmapur provided, I acted soon and could collect some evidence in this regard, I picked up a rifle and accompanied by two toughs, I left for Thakur P. N. Singh's farm on a jeep, from where I took a bullock cart and from there one hour's walk brought us to the water pond which the trader told me was the spot.

Here, I started my investigation and scanned the ground. The first thing I discovered, were the poacher's pits which were covered with leafy branches apparently to conceal them from the keen eyesight of the forest rangers. One was an old pit, it was located towards the west of the pond while the other was new, located slightly inside the tree line of the jungle. The latter was more strategically created and a hunter positioned here was sure to realize a better result. It appeared to be more popular amongst local poachers, for inside it I found a few dented copper caps that are used to fire the old muzzle loading guns. Sometime before some other poacher and not Ramu, who had used the old weapon must have unknowingly left them here after having used the pit for this purpose. As the pit was ideally situated I concluded that the poachers must have sat here on that fateful night.

I examined the area around the waterpond and gradually discovered the signs of tragedy. There were many dried patches of blood, all looking black and brown in colour, scattered in a restricted area around the waterhole. The sight bore obvious testimony to the gruesome incident. I counted 8 different points where the slaughtered ungulates, spilling their life fluid had fallen down. The spot where the tiger had slumped was more clearly marked as it showed a large quantity of coagulated blood stains. The poachers had worked smartly and they had readily removed the carcasses of all animals yet they did not seem to have taken care to eliminate these self-explanatory marks.

The atmosphere also seemed to retain a dull stench and at certain points around the pond it was more evident. I then set upon the difficult work of searching out the tiger's carcass, and all the time voicing my disgust beneath my breath, I loitered some distance in the jungle with my men and made an assiduous effort. I peeped at various probable spots in the hope of chancing upon a raised or uneven piece of land that might turn out to be the tiger's burial ground, using my nostrils to their utmost olfactory power. Towards late afternoon I began to feel tired but the tiger was not traceable. Finally, when the sun set and the light conditions worsened, I called it a day and deciding to resume my search the next day, I traced my steps back to the Thakur's grant where I had decided to stay the night. On the way we diverted a little and passed through Dharmapur. Here I stopped the cart and cleverly tried to inquire about the incident from some labourers. Nobody spoke a word about it. The people were far smarter than I had thought, they even denied the visit of Ramu to their village.

Now, in the absence of any tangible evidence, I was helpless and spent the night at the grant. Next day, Thakur called up two forest guards and a watcher. I took them to the sight of the occurrence and showed them the dried blood stains but to convince them that the particular cogulated blood belonged to the body of a tiger was difficult. The guards promised to work fast but despite the lapse of many days, nothing seemed to have happened. Though I made repeated requests to send the blood-stained soil sample for a laboratory examination, they were never taken seriously. The men concerned were casual yet they always kept assuring me that it would soon be done, as they had sent word to the headquarters and experts were expected to arrive at anytime. As if to justify my fears nobody ever came, probably no message had been communicated by field staff as a way of delaying tactics to help poachers to act quickly and remove howsoever little signs were still left at the site. I do not wish to comment here on the ambigious attitude of staff but I was so frustrated by their inaction that it was natural for me to arrive at such conclusions and above all such things do happen. Consequently, in my visit to the area after five days, the new development was that all the mud of the respective spots had been dug out rand pieces were broken and scattered here and there, so not even a single stain of any kind was left for me to work upon. This was surely the work of poachers who had once again learnt of my investigation in time and had taken good care to beat my efforts. At last the incident was registered just an ordinary case of poaching.

Due to my strong confidence in Uncle Blaster's previous performance I had forgotten to keep vigilance against the expected odds wherein the whole village had grown suspicious regarding my intentions and held me directly responsible for all the troubles. They had completely concealed the evidence of the dead tiger and also the other slain animals, then how could a man from Lucknow dare to investigate into the matter and ferret out evidence to convict them? There were a few recognised jail birds more prone to crime than others, and they started to keep a track on my activities and formulated an entirely new and different strategy to teach me a lesson. The method they had applied this time was not likely to cast any doubt on them. Subsequently, I went through a harrowing experience which could well have ended in a catastrophe had I not happened to carry my favourite Purdy shotgun in my hands.

(III)

Since my boyhood, I have had an immense liking for loitering around in the jungle. On occasions specially on moonlit nights for the observation and photography of animals I liked to sit on a *machan* at an ideal spot. Among nocturnal animals, the porcupine is very rarely to be seen. They rest in the dense grasslands and Sal forests, deeply ensconced in their burrows, and only come out after sunset to travel into the nearby fields in search of their food. They were quite numerous in the area and being frequent visitors to potato fields I knew that they would surely come out and a few of them may also stray out into my area and provide me with an opportunity to capture them on my camera. On that fateful day with the porcupine photograph in mind I had decided to spend yet another night sitting on a *machan* constructed in one of the most prosperous potato fields. As inwardly, I hoped that the chances of their arrival in this field were greater than any other place.

This area fell very close to the banks of Suheli river which at this time of the season was a shallow and lazy stream and its escarpment almost bare, largely devoid of any type of long grass. This absence of vegetation offered me a good view even across the river. This was the fortnight of bright moon. I knew that soon the light would be as good as the day light. I had brought a pocket-camera with an inbuilt flash light. From the standards of photography, though it is an inferior camera but having no other option I decided to make good use of it. An hour before sunset, I took-up my position on the *pokher* tree, with my back to a few small wattle huts that were facing the river and the jungle.

The sun sank in due course and while watching it, I listened to the sounds of the jungle which at all times have been pleasant music to my ear. The jungle moves into activity particularly at the close of the day, and again at dawn. Luckily both these times inclusive of the night hour, the jungle remains practically undisturbed and shows its completely truthful character whereas in the daylight hours, mainly because of the human infiltrators, the jungle does not seem to exhibit its real nature. The night hours actually offer a naturalist the best moments to understand the secretive world of woods, and the variety of calls rendered by the jungle inmates can always be the best source of information.

I have always been interested in jungle sounds for I believe that however proficient a naturalist may have become, there always exists enough scope for him to learn new things. In those days I considered myself partially quite ignorant in differentiating tonal circumflex of animal calls. It is not possible to interpret them until you first learn to recognize them. There are many joyous, casual, alarming, fearful and sad notes that reflect a variety of animal moods. Interestingly, jungle language is universal and all the different species, understand the signals given by each other. They also keep sharing important information about the movements of their predators, who generally emerge from their shelter in the darkness and prowl in search of prey throughout the night.

By the arrival of the day, my vigil which had proved quite rewarding for me came to an end. A pair of the porcupines venturing around my *machan* had literally posed many times for my camera providing me with a few standard photographs. The entire night I had also concentrated on listening to the different sounds of the jungle and in my attempts to decipher their meaning, I had taxed my faculty of imagination.

In the early morning hours, a herd of spotted deer comprising of females, and two families of Langoor monkeys had also shown up across the river, they leapt from branch to branch. Curiosity and playfulness were two attributes that seemed to me, to fit them completely. Their females and young first drank the water to their fill, meanwhile, a monkey watchman seated at the top of a *peepal* tree, discovered my presence and issued his staccato barking alarm cry. Immediately many members of the family cried in fear and apprehension, evidently because they could not see the source of danger within seconds along with the cheetals, they left the grounds and disappeared completely into the closeby bushes.

Their departure made me realize the time. It was almost 6 o'clock and my night job was already over. Having enjoyed a good time on the *machan*, I came down from it feeling all happy and satisfied, I pocketed my small camera and shouldering my shotgun, I trod my way back to the village over a beaten cart track.

The sun had began to ride in the sky and its warmth announced that yet another hot summer day was in progress. Big and small herds of cattle and goats were being driven by the herd boys. They were to be taken into the bush land across the Suheli river for the purpose of grazing. Watching and gesturing a friendly hello to many of these men, I walked for over two miles till I arrived at a place called Khalla.

Here at a distance of roughly 100 yards from the carttrack, stood an old *neem* tree, surrounded by a small cluster of bushes and casting its cool shadows on the ground just beneath this tree. Near its trunk I saw a big stud bull standing isolated, busily grazing the grass then by the side of the bull, a sudden human movement happened to catch my eye. Being curious I looked intently and saw the outline of a man lurking from behind the tree. At my sight, he slipped behind the trunk of the tree, it appeared as if he was trying to conceal his profile from my eyes. It was a deliberate act and I could not understand what had forced him to do so. The only visible part of his body were his hands, then I saw them working on the rope tied at the bull's neck. I thought that he was setting it free for the purpose of his convenient grazing.

This bull looked like the grandest of bovines I had ever seen. Feeling temporarily fascinated, I stopped to appreciate its huge body and the beautiful sweep of horns. At that time, I did not know that he was an extremely notorious and infamous rogue bull of this area.

I learnt later that he had killed two children and had injured several passers-by. As his unprovoked aggressions continued, the resident people made repeated protests to eliminate him, but owing to the religious Hindu sentiments in which the whole cow family occupies a very revered position, the idea of killing the bull was not entertained. Finally, its owner who evidently belonged to Dharmapur decided to keep the bull locked in the pen at his house. He was to be released only in the mating season to court with the cows and then at the end of the season he was to be locked again for a long time.

Now, as I was admiring the bull I suddenly heard him giving a terrible snort. For a moment he looked at me intently, the great sweep of his horns impressively swayed in the air and raising a small cloud of dust, he pounded his hooves on the ground. Then his head went down and he charged upon me. At first, I failed to understand whether it was a genuine or a mock charge but as the bull thunderously closed upon me I realised he had targeted me and then I was able to comprehend the severity of the situation. I acted fast and the next moment saw me bolting madly for safety. I entered the nearby sugarcane crop and ran between its short furrows, hoping to be able to dodge the huge bovine, but the bull entered the field from the exact point where I had entered it and came all out for me. He crushed and broke down the standing canes by the sheer force of his body and massive spread of his horns. Even in the dense cane crop his speed was considerable. Running in a zig-zag manner I hastily crossed the field and came out in the open. Here, I must have run some 10 to 15 yards when I saw the bull galloping out of the field in the open. Now I pulled up more and more power in my abdomen and ran with a speed I had never thought myself capable of attaining but still the bull with a show of unabated vigour continued after me.

In such moments of tense anxiety, a man's mind either works very fast or stops working altogether. Luckily, boxing had been my favourite sport in college days and I had learnt the foremost lesson of the ring, that the quickest possible decision in a bout always renders the initiator superior to his antagonist. So, with a momentary feeling that I was once again back in the ring with an entirely different and toughest ever rival, I decided to execute the most suitable counter action. The next moment I found myself prepared to gun down the bull regardless of Hindu sentiments and the fact of his being domesticated. I stopped, turned and aligned my gun. The beast offered little chance of a bullet hitting it at any vital spot. His shoulders were covered by his enormous horns, and his nose was thrust out straight ahead. There was no time to aim and there was no margin for error either I fired both the barrels of the shotgun almost simultaneously. At that moment he was, as measured later, only six yards away from me. On receiving the full charge of the metal, he stumbled onto the ground, but still the momentum of his body carried him forward and when he finally collapsed in a cloud of dust, he was hardly a meter and a half away from me, so much so that the torrent of blood gushing out his nostrils had splashed my trousers and feet.

Hastily, I reloaded the gun but there seemed no necessity for a repeater shot. The bull had slumped on the parapet, emitting gurgling sounds from his choking throat. Actually, the pellets of the number one Sailor Ballet Bird, shot at such a close distance of six yards had speeded forth in a consolidated, compact bunch, to work like a ball slug. They had buried themselves in the bull's brain and in the region of the heart inflicting a truly mortal injury at the beast.

Having recovered my breath I examined the bull, blood rapidly gushing out of his wounds while his motionless body lay on the earth in a ploughed wheat field amidst the clouds of the dust that had slowly begun to resettle on the ground. To all intents and purposes he had died on the spot.

All this rumpus had attracted the attention of farmers, who while working in their fields had witnessed the scenario from there. Many of them ran to my rescue shouting lustily to discourage the offending bull and also to assure me of their help. I shouted back to them to take it easy as I had already shot down the bull and he was stone dead.

I moved a little away from the bull and sat on the parapet of a maize field to recover. My nerves had become tense with this harrowing experience so I lit a cigarette with trembling hands. Even after some deep puffs I still did not feel composed enough to answer the innumerable queries being continuously put forth by the witnesses. Then, I found Thakur's old servant Roshan appearing from in between the crowd. He, while working in the neighbouring field had also observed the complete proceedings. He came to my rescue and asking me to relax he began to answer the questions at great length. He castigated and blamed Dharmapur people for this incident. The crowd heard him with curiosity and many of the men also nodded their heads in approval. Later, when my tension subsided and my thinking also steadied, I realized that my stay here in the field was not advisable at all, the news of the bull having been killed by me must have reached Dharmapur by now and from there the hoardes of villagers were expected to arrive at any moment. They could misbehave with me and under a strong pretext of religious blasphemy, they could easily harass, intimidate and as the advantage was on their side they could even try to assault me and under all likely probabilities, I would be absolutely helpless to resist their offence until I make use of my gun against them and take the law in my hands. So it was better to move out of here, before the mob arrives and the complications begin.

I came back to Thakur's house and told him what had happened. I found that the fellow became a bit nervous on this news, he assured me that he would tackle the situation but it would be still better if I also call my uncle from Larti. So losing no time, I despatched a runner for Mailani with the information, requesting my uncle to come as soon as possible.

Towards evening, motoring all the way down, "Uncle Blaster" duly arrived at the grant. This time, besides his usual army of ruffians he had also brought along his pack of a dozen hounds. First he went to examine the spot of the happening, where the bull still lay in the ploughed field and a congregation of vultures had settled upon it. The great scraggy neck creatures honked and struggled amidst themselves in their indefinable endeavours to tear apart a few more portions of flesh and then gulp it down avaraciously. Nearly half of the bull had already been devoured. Many old and frail looking birds were sitting around the corpse, unable to struggle with their strong companions. They were waiting for their turn to arrive, as I looked at the rapidly disappearing carcass, I wondered at the insatiable hunger of these birds, they are the synonyms of death for they live on it and show how impermanent the world is.

When the inspection part was over, the men quickly set upon their fact finding mission of how this could have happened. The notorious village was not far from this sight. Uncle

Blaster stood on the bonnet of his jeep and made an orientation of his goons as how not to take law in their hands and still sound terrible, Uncle Blaster gave them a piece of his mind, a tactful drama was enacted. At first two village curs were shot dead. This immediately created the desired impression, and a few prime suspects were nabbed and dragged out of their houses. They were made to stand inside the ring of furiously barking hounds. The dogs had received a wonderful training, their faces contorted hideously and they growled and barked with all the strength of their lungs. Intermittently, they also closed upon their quarry to give him an impression of pouncing yet they never touched them at all. This method soon broke down the spirit of men and a startling revelation of a plot to kill me came out on the surface. A labourer called Beera who also had a past criminal record was found guilty of the offence, although he kept attributing the mishap to an accidental folly and pleaded innocence, but my uncle refused to acknowledge it. The evidence clearly proved that it was a deliberate and intentional act and as soon as the truth was established Uncle Blaster in his typical feudalistic justice spelt out a penalty for Beera. He was primarily held responsible for the death of the bull and was told to throw a vegetarian feast to over hundred people in the village to repent his misdeeds. He was advised to live on alms for seven days as this was to help him to absolve his sins.

The village chief was also unhappy with Beera and seeing the atmosphere was congenial to settle some old scores he was nurturing in his heart, he also imposed a heavy punishment on him. Since it was not possible to execute it one time so it was imposed on him in several instalments. Faced by his limited options Thakur P. N. Singh also felt compelled to intervene. He did not want matters to get hard to settle as he had to stay here amidst these villagers, so a compromise was much in his own interest. He happily acted as a mediator between us and accomplished the task and the matter was disposed off and forgotten.

There is not much more to be told after this but the most significant thing noticed by the villagers was that many seasons passed one after another yet the saintly tiger never returned to his favourite haunt. Many people fondly remembered him and narrated his tales to their children, assuring them to wait for his reappearance. All of them waited in vain, for they never knew that their noble friend had already been claimed by the father and son duo of poachers.

5

The Business of Poaching

(I)

Yogesh and I have together visited over a dozen national parks and several reserve forests of India. In the course of all our travels, we made it a point to inquire about the poaching activities prevalent in the region and the details of methods applied to kill game by local hunters. In this process, we learnt about many methods of poaching and collected so much material that when I finally wrote all of it down, it was in itself worth enough to create an exclusive handbook on poachers and their ways. Later I prepared a lengthy report and submitted it for publication to the Lucknow edition of The Times of India in the summer of 1990. It was duly entertained and appeared in two large instalments. A major part of this article included the details about the poisoning and killing of tigers in Dudhwa by inhabitants of the region. By sheer factor of fortune, my report got support from a photograph which was supplied to the newspaper's editor by a person unknown to me, in connection with some other article which was perhaps not used by the paper. The photograph showed three fresh skins of tigers being dried in a secret hideout of poachers at Dudhwa National Park. This was a bold exposure indeed and I anticipated landing in trouble with any of the gangs of poachers that are active all the year round in the Terai, but nothing of the sort happened. Contrary to my anticipation, however, I landed in trouble with the forest department itself. The report created a flutter in administrative quarters. Spoiling tea sessions of many forest officials in the morning, the Minister in-charge of forests and environment immediately

summoned the secretary of the forest department to seek an explanation from him. He, in turn made a trunk call to the authorities of Dudhwa Park who motored down all the way to Lucknow. They collected my address from the newspaper's office and arrived at my residence. After a formal introduction they set upon a long and tiring session of questioning me, seeking several unnecessary and irrelevant answers from me.

What followed next was a gruelling and uncomfortable time for me. The officials, instead of seeking details of the poaching methods mentioned in my article only wanted to know from where had I got that photograph. I just kept wondering what I had done to displease the authorities, since they were rude and arrogant with me. There was only one gentleman among them named H.B. Srivastava, who was polite and reasonable. He himself had recovered a tiger skin from the possession of two poachers a month ago, and perhaps he believed that I was a wildlife lover and not a poacher. The other officials threatened to drag me to court in a case of aiding poaching or implicate me in some other case if I did not tell them where I had procured the picture. All my protests and explanations were in vain. I preferred to maintain a low profile and endured all their bluster. In the coming months, this evidence created a lot of other problems for me, but I will not bother my readers with needless details. It is sufficient to say that although the matter was closed for the time being, the shadow of suspicion over me persisted.

I have no hesitation in saying even now that considerable poaching is still taking place in Dudhwa area and instead of combating it in a determined and effective way, the authorities seem more interested in suppressing the news about it. Here I am reproducing that report for the benefit of my readers with just a few formal and minor modifications.

All I wish to suggest is that the government must introduce the concept of honorary wardens in all the parks who, bestowed with adequate authority, would be able to check poaching as well as keep a vigilant eye on the officials who neglect their duties or collude with the anti-socials.

At the turn of this century, the Indian subcontinent was one of the most rewarding regions in the world for an ardent big game hunter. The whole of this area served as an excellent reservoir for a great diversity of wildlife. If you place a world map on the table and run your finger on it from Afghanistan to Borneo, you will see that between these points lies a great stretch of land that is approximately one-eighth of the total globe. It includes many countries of Asia, namely Pakistan, Nepal, India, Burma, Bangladesh, Thailand, Malaya, Singapore, Cambodia, Indonesia and the isolated island of Sri Lanka. This great area comprises a variety of terrain. There are towering ranges of mountains like Hindukush, the Himalayas, Satpura, Nilgiris, Aravali and many others, the grand plateaus, vast regions of virgin jungles, parched deserts, evergreen rain forests, rambling hill countries and stately rivers like Indus, Brahmaputra, Ganga, Yamuna, Iravadi, Narmada, Krishna and Kaveri, etc. These rivers are born out of the melting glaciers and lofty snow covers in the Himalayan region. As they race down to the foothills of Terai, they are joined by many big and small mountain rivulets. In their east and southward flow, they gather force for their long and circuitous journey to the Bay of Bengal and to the Indian Ocean.

Nowhere in the world existed such a wilderness and a collection of wild animals so big, so numerous and so powerful. Its only serious rivals were east and central Africa. This subcontinent had all the four major predators: tiger, lion, leopard and cheetah. No tigers are found in Africa. In the African list of big game they had only five animals: lion, rhino, buffalo, elephant and leopard whereas in the Asian region, there were all these with three more, namely tiger, gaur and two species of bear, namely, Himalayan bear and sloth bear. Thus India had eight, which was the biggest number of Big-Game Animals in any single country. There were fourteen species of antelopes, wild goats and sheep, in mountains and plains, offering the finest stalking in the world. Africa had only one deer, the barbary stag, whereas India on the other hand had nine species of antlers or deer. Indeed there was no country in the world which could boast of such a wide range of game as the Indian subcontinent. Many sportsmen considered that hunting in India was far superior to that in Africa. It was hard and tough in comparison to African sport. Every trophy gained in the impenetrable dark jungles was richly earned by the sportsmen through toil, sweat and hard labour.

In those days, it was the natural ambition of a sportsman to test his skill, nerves and marksmanship upon a tiger and gratify his lifetime's ambition. There were a number of ardent hunters, both Indian and British, who spent many years in the jungle in a quest for tigers. There were many Maharajas who had made tiger-hunting a sort of a false symbol of status even though this sport was limited as a right of the privileged class. Unfortunately this class nurtured a high carnivorous instinct to kill more and more animals. Hunting became almost an obsession with Maharajas and in certain notorious individuals it even developed into a mania. There was such an intense and devastating competition to kill as many tigers amongst hunters that it resulted in a mass elimination campaign for tigers. Such men, in their egregious lust to enhance the number of killings could not remain averse to include newly born cubs or even unborn foetus in their bags. A certain Maharaja was credited to have killed eight tigers in a single rifle shot. It is simple to understand that he had shot a tigress which had seven foetuses in her womb.

Now if the Maharaja of Rewa claimed over five hundred tigers, then how on earth could the Maharaja of Udaipur lag behind? Working recklessly, he procured over a thousand of the species. But the great Maharaja of Surguja proved the most notorious of all. He surpassed all his contemporary rivals with a colossal number of over twelve hundred tigers to his credit. This Maharaja possessed only one serviceable eye. It is said that while on his *shikar* expeditions, the Maharaja used to get excited even at the sight of cheetal stag and there was nobody who could put a check on him from indulging in a relentless shooting spree. Once his friends dared to advise him to curtail this habit and the Maharaja perhaps in one of his saner moments, agreed to the proposal and vowed not to shoot over one thousand tigers. This target was agreeably approved by his friends as at that time, he was short of that figure by very small number. The Maharaja, however, accomplished the task of achieving the mark within a remarkably short time. The achievement was marked by a celebration and the Maharaja himself announced his retirement from tiger hunting.

He shifted to hunting lesser game to which he stuck for a few months. But it offered little or almost no thrill for the adventure-starved Maharaja. Then one day, he went out on a black buck shoot when a tiger emerged on the scene. The Maharaja eyed him greedily, but however, he was immediately reminded by his courtiers not to shoot the animal yet the man was very excited. He was repeatedly aligning his rifle on the sauntering beast but every time he was reminded of his promise. Meanwhile, the tiger had already crossed the open ground and was about to disappear in the *dhak* woods. The poor Maharaja was still undecided whether to shoot it or not to shoot, when suddenly his urge to kill won over him. He grew very angry with his courtier. He slapped him hard on his face and said, "Yes I had vowed to count up to one thousand tigers, so what? But from today I will not count them. You silly idiot, sit down and shut up." Then the Maharaja's rifle cracked and the striped form of the big cat went down to the bang of his gun. The Maharaja then continued this sport till the fag end of his life, having included around two hundred additional tigers in his bag of a thousand.

Massive deforestation has also been responsible for the declining fauna. During the British rule, the forest area mark was estimated to be around 35 per cent of the total land area against 9 per cent of the present times. Besides reserve forests in colonial territories, each and every state had a sanctuary of its own where some areas were completely prohibited from hunting. Actually, these were the sustainable zones that played an important role in maintenance of an abundant supply of game to the entire sanctuary.

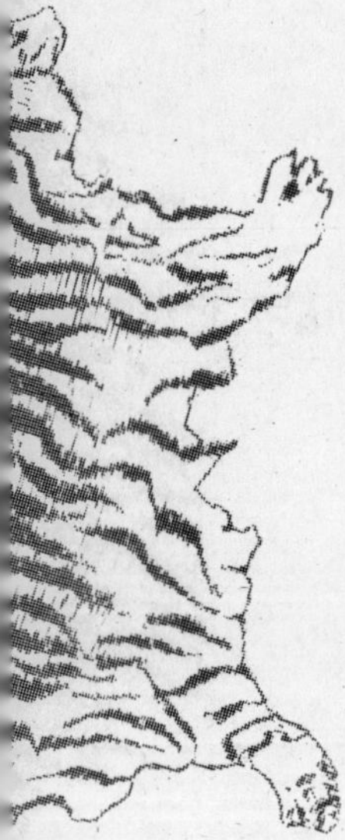

If the forests are eradicated then thousands of animals are condemned to death. Forests are cool and shady shelters that serve a variety of animal life as suitable breeding ground and also as their hunting grounds. With the advent of Indian independence, a great tragedy struck when India was divided into two parts. Great hordes of refugees arrived into India from Pakistan. As there was no land available for them to settle afresh, seemingly endless forests of Terai fell victim to the refugee rehabilitation plan of the government. A massive erosion of animal habitat took place and for years and years the woodcutter's axe resounded in the forest to provide refugees with settlements and means of their subsistence. Great jungles and great plains of grasses were replaced by cultivation fields. The men finally settled down as farmers. Agricultural yield in the Terai was tremendously rich but the depredation of great herds of deer and wild pigs that came out of the jungle in night was no less severe. They destroyed a large proportion of this production. Every effort was made by the government to curtail this pillage.

Gun licences for crop protection were issued to farmers on a massive scale. It benefited not only *bona fide* farmers but also came as a windfall for every Tom, Dick and Harry. Petty criminals, jail birds and hoodlums could count on getting a licence. We foolishly thought that once all the migrants are happily settled, a new era of peace and prosperity would dawn upon the Indian horizon. There was no law to control shooting outside the forest with the result that the guns that were provided for crop protection, necessarily armed the bands of poachers who slaughtered deer on a massive scale and began to sell their meat.

On every side the forest was still being cut down and destroyed. The marshes and lakes that harboured the grand concentration of game birds and were home of wild boars, sounders and swamp deer herds, were drained and put under cultivation. The speedy process of industrialisation left little hope for the wild animals to find cover to protect themselves. The ravages of the neo-hunter *viz*, the poacher, who justified his misdeed by calling himself a crop protector, continued and a new kind of hunting came into existence. This poaching, combined with the spread of cultivation and with the presence of ubiquitous cattle threatened the very existence of wild life. There was no buffer zone between the cultivation of field and jungle to prevent the clash between wild animals and human beings. The direct infiltration of man and animals into each other's zone finally proved calamitous for the animals only. Poaching continued unabated. The number of all kinds of animals reduced, their decline was brutally accelerated by the rifle-shooters. The rifle is the most destructive weapon in the jungle with its range exceeding over 100 meters. Animals within that range generally avoid human presence, thus automatically making the shotgun useless for their slaying.

The first beast to fall in this list of casualities was indubitably the tiger. No animal had been so consistently hunted than this battered predator. Nearly 42,000 tigers were estimated to have dwelt in the Indian jungles at the beginning of this century. This sounds a very large number but we must bear in mind that in relation to very large herds of deer, all of which form the tiger's natural prey, a population of 42,000 tigers was not all that stupendous.

In 1972, a proper scientific census for the first time was conducted by forest experts. The methods were based on three basic principles: First; every male tiger has a well defined territory, second; every tiger has a distinctive pug mark and third; the tigers or the tiger family drinks at least four times in a week.

This census brought out alarming figures. The number of this mighty beast had dwindled down to a mere 1800. An incredible number of over 40,000 tigers had been slaughtered by record settlers such as the Maharajas, bureaucrats, professionals and of course, poachers. Many naturalists were greatly sceptical about this figure. They questioned the reliability of methods involved in counting. The unproficient staff with little knowledge and inadequate instruments and with a poor knowledge of figures and the tiger's ways, was not averse to counting one number all over again for four times. Here it would be much in context to mention one of my very own experiences. A couple of years ago, my friend R.K. Shukla was Director of Lucknow zoo, and with his help I took plaster of paris casts of four tigers in the Lucknow zoo. I took the casts to the Dudhwa Park field staff. They studied them and declared them to be the pug mark casts of no less than a dozen tigers. Thus, the count given by the researchers were in fact wild estimates. The situation was even grimmer and the message was self-explanatory. The animal was fast heading towards extinction. The startling conclusion disappointed naturalists, who called for an urgent protection of this animal together with its environment.

A call was given by the international forum. Leading organizations namely International Union for Conservation of Nature (I.U.C.N.) and the World Wild life Fund (W.W.F.) got activated. In the process, more information about tigers was sought. Many projects were launched all over the wild regions of India to study in depth the various reasons for the near extinction of this animal and his habitat. The researchers worked on a war footing whereas other organisations endeavoured to raise funds to meet the expenditures of projects. Within a week, a fund of 1,75,000 dollars was raised to help the striped cat. Protests against its hunting were organised. In London, the activists even burnt down long coats made of tiger skin. With this interest on the international scene, the matter became of urgent concern for the Indian government. The then Prime Minister Indira Gandhi welcomed the idea of conserving wildlife and governmental action began in two ways. The first was to protect wildlife through propaganda and second was to impose a blanket ban on hunting through legislation. Finally, all these efforts ushered in a period for the rehabilitation of the tiger.

I hope I shall be proved wrong in saying that the government endeavours to save wildlife existed only on paper. The new regulations were incomplete and had apparent lapses in their implementation. The reports announcing an increase in wildlife population are still highly misguiding. The blanket ban on legitimate hunting actually opened the doors for illegitimate hunters, and encouraged them to continue their nefarious activities more easily and on a much more extensive and large scale as they had never done before. I can recall a great number of cases pertaining to poaching I have both witnessed and known which would, no doubt serve as an eye opener to my readers.

I believe that previously, the hunters who secured regular permits for shooting cannot be categorically blamed much for the deterioration in the number of wild life population. The majority of scrupulous sportsmen observed the rules and as a matter of fact they were never tired of acting as a strong check on poachers. These sportsmen wandered for great distances in search of game, diligently patrolling and scanning every nook and corner of the jungle and there was always a fair chance of discovery if there was any poaching activity in their area. They were rather the best watchmen of the jungle and for many of them a poacher was only the second best target after a tiger. They essentially reported the activities of poachers to the authorities to get them punished because it was in their own interest. For poachers, it was a difficult and highly dangerous proposition to embark into an area where a permit holder was known to be hunting, but the government regulations had banned hunting only for permit holders and not for the poachers.

With the absence of this alert tribe of watchmen, no serious contender was left to challenge the poachers. Thus, the atmosphere for poachers became better and more convenient to continue their pursuits. Now one has only to move in the jungles to perceive the intensity of poaching raids. Vehicles patrol the jungle roads at night with powerful spotlights and torches blazing and guns jutting-out in all directions to massacre the game. The females and young of all species are indiscriminately killed. Even big animals do not get a chance of survival against an armoury of guns fired simultaneously upon them. As the poachers are heavily armed with large and medium bore rifles and the fact that they are professionals, they are more akin to hardened criminals. By a curious paradox, the forest department is always understaffed. The game scouts and guards are poorly equipped with 12 bore shotguns that are remotely useful for long range encounters. The possibility of the guards being attacked by poachers is far greater than the latter facing any threat from the law. This generally keeps the forest staff demoralised.

(II)

Now, the successful penetration of poachers in sanctuaries and national parks is a matter of extreme regret. These are the

An adult tiger in the shadows of Sal trees.

A tiger in his typical habitat with a good view of water holes and prey trails.

Seeking respite from the scorching heat.

A tiger couple in their courtship period.

Adolesce

Solitary tiger on a hunt tyl
existence.

at play.

's life style of independent

A tigress reacting to the perceived threat. This one belongs to Mala Reserve forest of Pilibhit district.

Adolescent cubs exploring their natural habitat.

Overleaf
These pictures are from Corbett National Park, some moments before and after the kill. Notice the intensity of tiger's expression while stalking its prey.

A tiger out on a territorial prowl.

Picture showing varying patterns of marking on the face. Identifying the tiger with his pugmark supported by the facial marking is the most practical method of counting the tiger in the wild.

Sleeping ! actually quite alert to the possibilities of catching a prey.

Patrolling-an integral part of a tiger's life.

The best tuskers in National Parks have been killed by poachers. This one survives because of poor quality of its ivory.

A small herd making its migratary pilgrimage through the dried up river bed. They are most vulnerable at these times.

In Kaziranga and Manas reserves, nearly 1200 Rhinos have been slaughtered by local poachers.

The Indian marsh crocodile-another specimen of the wild living on the brink of extinction.

last resorts of wildlife and there considerable hunting is known to be conducted in connivance with authorities. Random investigations reveal that at many places the subordinate staff of the forest department as well as the police are involved in poaching activities. The field staff of both the departments has the natural advantage of coming in contact with the local populace, specially with the influential political or other heavyweights of the area whose cooperation they essentially seek to run the administration. These men, on a personal level develop intimate contacts with the staff and then, seek illegal favours. Corruption makes the soliciting even easier. They generally enter into a courteous honorable agreement—it is the responsibility of the field staff to guide their hunter friends into some safe and remote area where he can avail the opportunity and time to hunt as he desires. In the core pockets of national parks, where the game is still abundant, just the firing a few shots on any herd can ensure even a blind man with a couple of trophies. The staff also bears the responsibility to protect their poacher friends from the long arms of law, and the poachers, in turn, pay handsome amounts in cash and kind for this favour bestowed on them.

The other form of sport is hunting in the night with the aid of spotlights. It is a very popular sport when the lights are focussed on the eyes of the animal, he is temporarily obfuscated and stands as though hypnotized, offering himself as an easy target. The hunters take the opportunity and ruthlessly shower a volley of bullets on the animal regardless of whether they are shooting a male or female.

In national parks, the animal is quite used to seeing tourists. He does not run away at the sight of the poacher and mistaking them for harmless visitors, he subsequently falls an easy prey to his gun. Besides meat and skins, the magnificent horns of stags also fetch a very good price in the market. The states of Kashmir, Bengal and Tamil Nadu have certain defined districts which serve as a market for such horns. They are sold to the tourists at inordinate prices. The foreigners normally have a very poor knowledge about Indian animals. They do not hesitate in buying even grossly freak items created by inexperienced taxidermists.

Once , recently at a shop in Pahalgam, in the state of Jammu & Kashmir I happened to come across a stuffed head of a blue bull on which the horns of a spotted deer were mounted. A novice taxidermist seemed to have created this wonder but the shopkeeper considered it a rarity and expected to get a good price for it. Interestingly enough, there was an American couple already in the process of bargaining for this silly looking trophy. Feeling curious, I listened to the shop-talk wherein the dealer explained that the specimen was a rare one as it was the head of the progeny of a cross between a deer and an antelope. The Americans were convinced and were about to buy it when I intervened and told them the truth. The shopkeeper was furious and leaving all his customers he came out of the shop to settle scores with me for curtailing his profit. I was in no position to take him on, so, I immediately left the scene to avoid the bitter consequences.

My knowledge about poachers and their ways is largely based on my experiences obtained in the Terai Bhaber region of U.P. and Bihar. Here, I have watched how natives, whose quest for meat is continuous and to whom necessary weapons to kill the animals are rarely available are compelled to employ devilish methods to accomplish destruction of wild animals. The element of cruelty involved in these wicked practices is certain to stir up the anger and dislike of every sensible man; and the regrettable fact is that law is completely helpless to punish them.

Some of the more deadly methods are described in the following pages.

The usage of a crude bomb is by far the most commonly-employed method of killing animals. This awkward item is not difficult to manufacture, as it consists of miscellaneous things like small stones, flint chips, glass splinters and nails mixed with a large quantity of gunpowder. The mixture is later enclosed in a paperbag which is held together by a strong thread tied tightly all over it. Then once again glass splinters and small nails are stuck over the bag, and a second mixture of the explosive is repasted over it. This ball is then enclosed in a cloth bag and fastened all over again by the threads. Once the process is complete, the bomb is ready to use.

The explosive power of the bomb depends upon the quantity of material used in its preparation. The weight of bomb varies from 200 gm. to 900 gm. Smaller bombs are used for the lesser game, like stags, whereas the bigger ones are used for big games such as cats and other large animals. These bombs are coated with thick flour paste, over which the grass-shoots and grains are also affixed. This is done to attract the animals. By this trick, the chances of success are enhanced. The hunters carry these bombs into the jungle and places them at strategic points regularly visited by the animals. Salt licks, water-pools, game trails and lush green glades are the ideal spots for this purpose. In due course, some ill-fated animal arrives on scene attracted by the smell of the edible substance coated on the bomb. When to eat the grains the animals holds the bomb in his mouth and bites to crunch it, the pressure ignites the explosive powder. The bomb explodes and generally blows off the head of the animal. Once, while trailing the tracks of a man-eating tigress on the banks of Katna river on the border of Shahjehanpur and Kheri, Yogesh and I had come across a cheetal whose entire jaw was blown off by a crude bomb.

Another dreadful method freely practiced by the poachers is the application of dragnet. It is termed *khabar* in Terai region. A netting is woven out of thick ropes, it normally measures up to three metres in height and it can be of any length ranging from minimum of ten metres to the maximum of 40 metres. At the start of the hunting operations, these dragnets or *khabars* are spread in the forest at an inclination of sixty degrees to the land, abutting the trees. Once, over two decades back in my early teens, I had witnessed a complete hunting operation conducted by poachers, precisely Chhotey Pasi, my old jungle trainer of Larti and his gang, in which nets were profitably used to pile-up a handsome tail of ungulates.

In this form of hunting, the nets are hung by line of bipods, each of which consists of two strong bamboo poles set four feet apart on the ground. The bamboo poles are tied to the pegs. It is to prevent them from slipping and the net which hangs vertically from the apex of the bipodes is also secured with the pegs to prevent the animal escaping from under the net. It is a strange habit of wild animals that they never try to jump over the net. They rather attempt to slide through from beneath the net. At times, poachers with an intention to procure a great catch block vast areas of the jungle, ranging from 500 to 800 yards by joining several dragnets together. Then the beats begin. The herds of animals are driven towards the dragnets. Terrified, they dash and plunge into the nets. The more they try to free themselves the more and more firmly they are caught in the nettings.

At times, in beats of long distances, tigers and leopards are also cornered. But this does not worry poachers for they are safely placed to claim them and that too very easily. Actually when a disturbed tiger, escaping from the beaters, comes across human beings standing in the jungle, he attempts to take them through the nets and in the process he provides an excellent opportunity to poachers to spear him down.

Once the beat is over and the stag herds are caught, the ropes of the nets loosened. The net falls upon the animals, entangling them even more firmly, then the beaters arrive and start slaughtering the animals in a merciless and cruel manner. They use all kind of primitive weapons ranging from swords, spears, daggers, *lathis,* bows and arrows and even heavy stones to crush the animal's heads to dispose them of. At times, just in a single operation, several small herds of deer comprising three or four animals in each group may get entrapped. In this way, the number of animals thus caught may be as high as fifty. Such catches are indeed rewarding for poachers, but in the process they practically denude the forests for miles and miles, and after the operations are complete, no animals are found loitering there for many many weeks until the place of the killed animals is once again occupied by new migrant herds who too subsequently meet the fate of their predecessors.

This method is generally practiced by the businessmen who deal with the flesh of animals. In a village of Puranpur Tehsil of Pilibhit district, I have myself seen the flesh of spotted deer and hog deer being sold openly on a large scale. The clever butchers in an attempt to deceive the anti-poaching squad, tie a few goats in pegs around their shops as a ruse for selling the venison as mutton. The truth under the circumstances is never known as there is no apparent signs of any mischief. There must be hundreds of places in India where this trade is being secretly practised. It cannot be controlled until meat samples in all village markets of the jungle region are regularly collected and checked by experts. Otherwise, the practice is bound to continue unabated.

Next comes the wire snare. It is yet another highly gruesome method practiced by individual poachers. Here, a snare of thin iron wire is placed in between two trees at a place which is frequented by animals. As soon as the unfortunate creature walks through this space against the snares, they wreath his body quickly and tighten on his mouth, neck and haunches. His desperate attempt to free himself from this sudden trouble only results in getting him more firmly entangled into the killer snares. If the animal is big and strong, such as sambhar, blue bull or a swamp deer, it may break up the knots by powerful pulls and run away but this will not save his life for the lengthy wire already firmly tied to his body, trails behind him. It entwines and entangles with the trees and bushes that fall behind him in his escape. This hinders the running of the animal and the snares tighten around the vulnerable parts of his body and leave him utterly helpless for any activity. A severely injured beast with a tied mouth is not expected to eat his food or even drink a drop of water. Quite often the injured animal dies in the deep recesses of the jungle and its body decomposes there. Hunters are generally unable to locate it and the kill is atrophied. Sometimes the wire snares cut open the windpipe of the animal and make him suffer pangs of agonising pain. With blood dripping from his wounds all over the body, the animals presents a horribly grotesque picture and wanders madly in the jungle for several days, before ultimately dying a lingering and indescribable death.

The methods of dragnets and crude bombs though are immediately successful, but have a major shortcoming, in being a ceremony of sound, in themselves. They often reveal the hectic activities of poachers at their earliest stage. Beating of tom-toms to drive the animals and loud explosions are liable to bring them in a direct confrontation with the forest vigilance staff. Therefore, to continue their activities without trouble, the poachers use a quiet method of catching animals through trenches or pits, termed *khanti* in local parlance. The pit is approximately seven to eight feet deep, and five feet wide. They are dug in various parts of dense forest where normally the patrolling staff cannot reach by a cycle or jeep. The pits are carefully covered with grass and stems so that outwardly the ground over them appears even. Amid the grass, towards the centre, grain, paddy and straws of wheat, etc. are delicately placed.

Animals are attracted by the grains and as they attempt to eat it they fall into the pit. These pits are regularly checked by poachers and the animals trapped in them are killed with spears and blows of *lathis*. These pits serve as a permanent source of food to natives. Once they are built, they are there for months and ever useful except in the rainy season, when they are filled up by water and flowing mud. It is only then that they are to be re-excavated. They are a sure method of success and if by some reason, poachers fail to check the pit, the entrapped animal lies there helpless, and dies a painful death by thirst and starvation.

The story of the decline of Dudhwa National Park is no less sad. In the last decades of eighties, a sharp rise in tiger population was noticed in this area. The pressure mounted by the extent of increase compelled a fair number of tigers to migrate into the adjacent fields of sugarcanes, and an all-time high number of tigers was recorded in these fields.

In those years, around 40 tigers were estimated to be dwelling in the crops out of the regular jungle. The official records admit that these tigers spread sufficient terror in the border areas of the jungle. They attacked and killed cattle, intimidated field workers and even claimed an occasional human victim. Nevertheless, the natives regularly reported these cases to the forest department but the government machinery was so slow that it took months to respond to their grievances. The compensation given to the farmers for their killed cattlehead was inadequate and that too released after a lot of questions, arguments and canvassing. It was also not entirely unjustified as investigation done by the forest department showed that in a majority of such cases, the claims of the farmers were fraudulent. The cattle claimed to be killed by the tigers were frail and diseased. They were useless for any purpose except for being sold as beef. So the probability of their being killed by the villagers themselves to make it appear like a tiger kill could not be ruled out. This suspicion often lead to complications and denial of compensation to genuine sufferers in settlement of their claims. Subsequently, the situation turned volatile and a group of villagers decided not to inform the government in future about their losses but to deal with the scourge themselves. They decided to shoot the tiger no matter what may happen.

Certain maleficient elements also took advantage of the situation, but still it was not safe to lay hands on the tigers because they feared the leakage of the news. It could only be done with the cooperation of local inhabitants. They contacted the frustrated lot of villagers and instigated them to settle their scores with the tigers. I say this because I believe that a small-time poacher does so to care only for his stomach. They do not generally embark on big adventures such as a tiger killing, because it is of no use to them. It begins only when large poaching gangs offer them enough security and activate them into a big act. Some enterprising men do it independently while the others connive with the professional groups for nefarious deeds. The act in the end benefits both the parties, the local native gets rid of the scourge whereas the poachers get a skin to sell.

The operations were carried out secretly, the easiest method was to poison the predator to death. In Terai area, spraying of pesticides for crop protection is very prevalent as is the case all over the country. Hence, these chemicals are freely available to all the people. This spelt doom for the tiger. Whenever a cattlehead was killed by the tiger, the men sprayed these poisonous chemicals copiously on the carcass and even kept the semi-solid balls of this substance namely carbofuran, B.H.C. Gamma, Lindane, Lintaf and Hepta Chlore etc. inside the fleshy part of the animal. Later, when the tiger returned and fed upon his kill he inevitably became unconscious and due to the strong toxic effect, died within a few hours. In case his intake had been inadequate, he would only become unconscious but still he had no chance of survival as he was speared to death by the hunter, whose watchful eyes were on him.

The foresters, due to lack of evidence, are unable to punish the culprits. *Ear Peer,* this kind of tiger killing was almost unknown in Dudhwa area but since the advent of the eighties it was introduced and it continues. A Sikh farmer of the area was once emphatic in telling me that his men had killed not less than eight tigers and buried them somewhere in his field. "Don't ask me where they are now," he said. Even if some discount is given for his boast, he or his grooms must have killed at least one tiger surreptitiously, and that also counts.

These poachers had and still have, their secret hideouts in the jungle. The carcasses are transported to them where expert taxidermists skin the animal and then its flesh, fat, whiskers and bones all are transported to cities, hidden with miscellaneous cargo items to be utilized in various ways. In China, a supposedly potent wine for vitality is distilled from the predator's bone. In the later years of the eighties, close to the Majhegain range of Dudhwa reserve forest, two villages, namely Pattihan and Basantapur had earned notoriety for tiger killings. The inhabitants of these villages were known to have poisoned and killed at least six tigers that dwelt in the adjacent sugarcane fields. Then further on, the incident of Bhira range in South Kheri served as an eye-opener to the forest department, telling them what gruesome things had actually been happening in their area. On August 18, 1986, a young *kanjar,* (a member of a nomadic tribe), was intercepted by the police. He was carrying a cloth-covered basket tied to the carrier of his bicycle. The police forced him to open the basket in which the bones of five tigers were found. He was thoroughly interrogated and his disclosures were startling. He said that for the past several years, his community had been operating in this area and during this time they must have accounted for over 30 tigers. At present, they were completing a big assignment of supplying spotted deer skins and in the trans-Sharda area, many of his men were engaged in active hunting. The information was alarming and a raid was organised but it failed to yield any result as the smart poachers had already decamped from their hide-outs.

It was again on September 6th and 9th of the same year that carcasses of two tigers were found floating in the Sharda canal. It appeared that the poachers, after having killed the tigers were carrying them across the canal when their boats capsized and subsequently, the carcasses were washed away by the strong currents and were recovered at the Sharda dam. The autopsy of the carcasses revealed that the atrocious method of laying *jin* traps was used to kill these tigers. It was long considered that this method was not being applied in the area. A couple of years ago the anti-poaching squad of the park had organised a series of massive raids with the help of police during which 42 *jin* traps were confiscated from the peripheral villages. Since then, there had been a lull for a long time till the tiger corpses discovered in Sharda canal indicated that the wicked practice had been resumed once again.

Jin trap is the most dangerous of all the equipment used for the trapping of big cats. It is basically an iron apparatus made out of two independent parts. The first is the main trap which is up to four feet in length to both sizes of which are attached two big and strong springs. It is set in such a way that even the slightest pressure would cause the powerful saw-toothed jaws to snap shut on the part of the victim caught in it. The second part of trap is thick iron rods on which it is supported. Keeping in the view the size and strength of the animal that is to be hunted, the number of these rods can be increased from a minimum of four to a maximum of eight. The short and small rods separately weight from 10 to 30 kg. each. When they are joined in the main trap they construct a formidable device which may weight from 40 kg. to 150 kg. When it is put into use, the apparatus is buried into the ground except for its top jaw which, projecting out of the earth, is kept open with a piece of meat delicately placed inside it. This trick is sure to lure a carnivore into it. The trap is then placed on a regular beat frequented by big cats. It is placed in such a way that for the hunter's quarry, there is practically no way to avoid it.

Once the trap is ready, hunters sit and wait for the animals. In the night, some tiger or leopard hurrying down the path discovers the piece of flesh and is naturally attracted towards it. As he proceeds to collect the food, he inevitably puts its paw or mouth into the trap to steal the morsel and his efforts result in a sudden closing of both jaws. His paw is caught so firmly in the trap that despite his best endeavours, the cat is unable to free himself. When he attempts to pull out his paw the wicked nails deeply scratch his flesh, leaving him roaring and roaring in mortal pain till his spirits are completely broken. At last he lies panting and extremely exhausted, waiting in a patient resignation for the hunters to arrive and kill it.

Once, Billy Arjon Singh a noted conservationist, who lives near Dudhwa National Park had also found a tigress near his farm caught in a trap. Her milk teats were swollen, showing that she had cubs. Next day when he revisited the spot, he found the tigress missing from there. It appeared that she had either escaped the trap or the trapper's had probably taken her away. In case it was, then the cubs in their infancy would not have survived far long.

Next to it comes archery. It is still an esoteric form of sport in the remote areas. This weaponary is primitive, but its efficacy at close range cannot be subordinated by any quantum of charge fired by a shotgun. Natives consider it as one of the most effective weapons for doing battle and hunting. I consider myself lucky to have witnessed some of the finest examples of archery and I have no hesitation in saying that a skilled archer equipped with a high-quality bow and arrow can meet any of the six big game animals on his own terms.

Once in 1974, I had the occasion to accompany my grandfather, Pt. K.L. Shukla. He was then a Minister of Revenue in Madhya Pradesh Congress government on an inspection to the district of Jagdalpur. It is a heavily forested region of Bastar. During those days one of my paternal uncles, D.P. Shukla, was also posted there as district judge and another relative as commissioner. While we were putting up in the circuit house, we received news of a mischievous leopard who had been terrorising a village for a long time. This area is a stronghold of leopard population. They make a nuisance of themselves to the acute discomfort of the local inhabitants. In forest files up to 1960, they were classed as a vermin and their destruction was encouraged by the government. Their slayer was rewarded with a cash award of Rs. 20/-.

This leopard in question had killed 20 goats in a village in just one night. The goats were kept in a cattle pen when by midnight the leopard came and climbing over the barricade, jumped inside. Despite the terrific din created by goats, he stayed there for more than an hour and in an apparent lust for blood, had grounded all the 20 goats. The District Commissioner then passed orders for his execution. As per the order a local expert was to accompany the hunters. When my uncle asked for the right man, all the villagers volunteered to do the job. Showing us their bows and arrows, they tried to convince us that none of the villagers if chosen for this work, will ever fail to slaughter the beast with these weapons. Infact, in my childhood days I had witnessed some excellent demonstrations of archery at my ancestral village, Larti, in Mailani but I had never imagined that it could also be effectively used against big game animals. I expressed my doubts and thought the statement was overfluous. This excited an old man. He asked us if we would like to see the striking power of his arrows. Then, without waiting for our answer, he went to the nearest house and returned with a stout domestic boar. He left the animal free at a distance of 15 yards and asked his son, who was standing there with his bow, to fire an arrow on it and show what miracle it can do. His son was a short and sturdy person and seemed to possess bovine strength in his body.

The man placed his shoulder-high bow on the ground and pulling it with all his muscle power released an arrow. It zoomed through the air and in the very first strike, its shaft crossed through the thick body of the boar and protruded on the other side. The boar ran for his life but a rapidly following volley of arrows knocked him down on the ground. I was deeply impressed by the performance. Later, I examined the bow. It was made of a high quality wood superbly embellished and all the arrows were long and fine with perfectly balanced metallic shafts.

The performance had been outstanding but owing to the legal lacuna, no archer was assigned with the job. The leopard was finally shot down by a game scout, but he had to spend a long time on its trail and one of his men was also badly mauled by the beast, but that is in a different context.

The nomadic tribe of *kanjars,* about whom I have nominally mentioned in the previous pages of this chapter, is in fact a potential menace to wild fauna. They are absolutely illiterate and stubborn. No amount of debate or arguments can convince them of the importance of environment protection, conservation and ecology. The only explanation that can be offered for this incorrigible behaviour is that from times immemorial their subsistence has always rested on the flesh and skin of wild animals. Having no hereditary training in any other profession they are unskilled except for hunting. They cause a great damage to wildlife that once their raids are over, practically every vestige of game disappears from the affected area and it remains denuded of game for quite a long time.

To strengthen my statement, I would like to describe one of the extremely dexterous hunts that I had witnessed in my boyhood.

In the winter of 1970, an American called John Allen had come to India to shoot tigers. Mamman Khan who was then serving as a professional hunter in a hunting firm of Delhi called India Shikar and Tours Private Limited, had been entrusted with the responsibility of the shoot. He had taken care to reserve Motipur shooting block of Bahraich in advance for him. Mamman Uncle, as I cali him, had cordially invited me to participate in this shoot. The offer was too tempting for me to refuse so I packed my luggage and accompanied the shooting party to Bahraich. On the fifth day of our stay at Motipur, Allen shot down his tiger. The achievement was good but since it had culminated so early, it had lessened the thrilling attraction of the hunt. With the tiger hunt having already been accomplished, we directed ourselves in search of antelope and stag heads and wild boar trophies. According to local information, a few great wild boar sounders dwelt in the area, and some of their leaders carried curved tuskes upto eight to ten inches long. The hunt turned out to be highly rewarding and in a week's time we succeeded in procuring two sambhars, six spotted deers, one bear, two *kakars* and one leopard but at this time, the wild boars seemed to elude us. Despite our frantic search for days and nights, we failed to locate even a single boar.

One day, in the early morning we got information that a sounder containing over a dozen heads and supported by two massive males was sighted in an agricultural field. We hurried after it and an hour later, we found ourselves trailing on the tracks on the wild boars. The trail started from the field, and took us to the jungle and as once again we neared the forest, at its periphery we encountered a newly erected camp of *kanjars*. The very first sight of the camp agitated Mamman Uncle. "Bloody killers", he murmured with a sore heart. "They have come here to indulge in savagery," he said and turned to the American to tell him that we should better forget all about sport." The jungle is theirs as long as they stay here, and I am sure they will not leave any moving thing alive." He in fact wanted to report about their arrival to the forest security staff but the American tourist stopped him from doing him so. He was impelled with a curiosity, and desire to know about their life-style and culture, rather than seeing them being driven away. More than that, if possible, he wanted to witness their traditional methods of hunting various animals. Allen insisted that we contact them, mentioning that they would be paid handsomely if they gave a practical demonstration of their hunting techniques.

In fact, under all circumstances, a professional hunter has to accomodate for the satisfaction of his client who is paying him good money to get all the thrills and sensations of the wilds. Mamman agreed to the proposal and stopped the jeep and from there, approached the site of the camp. At the opening of one tent, we saw the skins of rabbits, foxes, cats, mongoose, and jackals being dried in the sun. They hung on a stretched rope that was supported by two poles. A couple of dogs loitered around the camp while the male members of the tribe stood assembled in the centre of the site, excitedly involved in a discussion about the probability of game they hoped to catch in this area. We reached the spot and introduced ourselves as the customers of skins. Then a brief conversation followed and soon both of us befriended them. When we requested them to show us their hunting style the party readily allowed us to accompany them, as they were just leaving for a jackal hunt. We were obliged to receive this invitation. The American was also included. The hunters armed themselves with daggers and spears and then, accompanied by all the dogs of the camp, we proceeded for the jungle.

Incidently, in the context of East Bengal, this type of jackal hunting has also been described by Augusts Somervile in his wonderful book 'The Passing off the Forest Gods' and I have also read in media reports about this method being practiced in Karnataka and Orissa. Now when I analyse the incident after a long experience I naturally conclude that the hunting methods of different *kanjar* tribes are quite similar. It is due to their bearing of original primitive acceptance no matter whatever or howsoever distant may be the geographical regions of their operation.

As we reached inside the forest, we searched for an ideal spot for the hunt. Finally, a *nallah* which held a small rill of seasonal water together with a thick cluster of bushes at its corner was chosen for this purpose.

The hunters set upon their work. At first, two nomads with their four massive and extraordinary strong looking dogs went inside down a cluster and thoroughly concealed themselves within it with the help of leaves, twigs and other miscellaneous forest materials. While the remaining one along with their dogs walked into the close by forest and posted themselves at strategic points, forming a broken ring around the glade. From here, they could keep a watch on the cluster and stay ready for action. There were no animals in sight and I was unaware of the kind of hunting they were going to perform. An old *kanjar* eradicated my doubts and told me his men will call the game here if it happens to be anywhere in the jungle within the hearing range of their calls. I could sense that it was going to be an interesting affair. Later, the old *kanjar* also disappeared into the woods and all three of us perched ourselves on the branches of a tree that stood at the edge of the clearing.

From this vantage point, I could get a suitable view of the

whole clearing. A few minutes later the hunt commenced. A mournful howl slowly rose from the cluster, increasing gradually in volume. The sounds resembled the intrinsic calls of jackals that are produced at the sight of food. The call was repeated ten to twelve times at brief intervals and then it changed into a miserable yelping. Suddenly, a variety of sounds rose into the atmosphere and soon, the din created by jackals fighting amongst themselves could be heard all around in the cluster. It seemed as if a haranguing scuffle had broken out between the two jackals over a succulent morsel. The contrived fight was so realistic and convincing that if I had not known that these cries were emanating from the nomads hiding in the bushes, I would have been taken in to believe that a group of jackals was making them. Even the jackals believed them to be coming from their own ilk, as I was later to witness.

The sounds rose to an orgasm of yeh...yeh...yeh...yeh and continued for about ten minutes. Then I sighted four jackals emerging from the eastern side of the forest. They hurried towards the *nallah* in anticipation of obtaining some food. A lone jackal came from the opposite direction and was first to dash madly into the *nallah* where the hunters were waiting for their quarry to arrive, to oblige them with a killing strike. As the jackals entered, the hunters unleashed their dogs who recklessly pounced upon the helpless scavengers with a rush. Realising that it was an ambush, the jackals took to precipitate fight but they were granted no opportunity to do so, because at the same moment the men who were hiding behind the trees let loose their dogs too. The dog squad was superbly trained. Working in excellent coordination they caught hold of all the jackals and came there lifting them by the scruff of their necks while all their the four paws moved freely in the air, the obedient pack of pets returned to their masters who systematically put the victims to death.

The catch was enough for the day and that very afternoon, five more fresh skins of jackals were stretched on the iron pegs and hung on strings for drying, outside the tents of the nomads, while the blood- stained odious remains of homicide were simply thrown at the countryside. The vultures soon dropped upon them. It was interesting to note that though the camp dogs, who had slaughtered them, hung around the carcasses, probably because of a repugnant odour showed no inclination to eat them.

Later that evening the American client succeeded in shooting down two wild boars probably from the same sounder we had been following since morning but they turned out to be very poor specimens. In the waning light conditions, the great master boars escaped into the hedges before a shot could be tried on them. This left the American disappointed. A day after this shooting, the period of our hunting permit was over, so we packed our belongings and came back to Lucknow. While on our way back, we did not see the *kanjar* camp again. They had probably migrated to some other area in search of more game. A similar technique is also applied to call foxes, wolves and a variety of lesser cats, and they are slaughtered in an identical manner.

Today, the black buck is on the verge of extinction and if this happens, the world would have lost one of its most spectacular antelopes. Just a few decades back there were plenty in the plains just like the spotted deer. Great herds of black buck roamed the wasteland all over the peninsula. I remember the days in my childhood when, in the early sixties on the highways from Lucknow to Barabanki and from Lucknow to Sitapur, several black buck herds along with blue bulls could be seen browsing by the side of the roads. In the same decade villagers were given gun licences to protect their crops from raiding black bucks. This accelerated the process of their slaughter. In fact the slaughter was pursued so relentlessly that great herds completely disappeared from these areas. At present, not even a single black buck can be seen for hundred of miles in this area. Scattered herds of blue bulls can still be found roaming in the fields mercifully spared from the onslaught because of certain religious sentiments of Hindu masses towards them.

The last concentrations of black buck exist in Gujarat with their backs against the wall, they are waging a struggle for survival against the ravages of the poachers that continue to attack them. The digestion process of a black buck is complicated. They belong to family called Bovidie and an order of the antelopes that being ruminates, chew the cud, partially masticating it. The animal first swallows the food with a preliminary munching and then sits in the shade to digest it. With the commencement of the digestion process, the food is pushed up from stomach by the gastronomical pressure to the mouth for the supplemental mastication before being finally swallowed. During this period of second mastication, the antelopes become highly incapable of sudden precipitate and protracted movement. If it is put on a run by beats or by sheer chasing, the helpless animal is quickly exhausted. The knowledgeable poachers have a fair idea as to exactly when the second digestive process would begin and for how long it would last. They observe the herds feeding, then calculate the time by when they would retire for resting. They wait till the right moment and release the packs of hunting dogs after them.

A black buck with light food in his stomach is estimated to attain a speed up to sixty miles per hour and once put to flight, they would continue at a steady pace and maintain their speed mile after mile, breaking the spirit of the most dogged pursuers. With a full stomach and especially in the event of second mastication, his speed is considerably reduced. As the dogs go inexorably after the bucks, the hunters follow them with their bows, arrows, spears and bamboo staves. The young fawns are the first to fall for they are unable to sustain the long running. Females also exhaust quickly and collapse on the ground, subsequently, they are torn to shreds by the attacking dogs or caught by the men who bundle them with the savage blows of spears and staves. Male black bucks normally have a great stamina despite being burdened with the digesting process. They have a sufficient reserve of energy to carry themselves far away from danger, and they are the only survivors in the great chase.

The poor male antelopes are doomed before the wily poachers, who have yet another fool-proof method of catching them by fishing hooks. Their chief interest lies in his long spiral horns and the gorgeous black and white coat that is most conspicuous of this genus and sells at a handsome price.

Antelopes are very fond of eating a small fruit called *kachara*. It grows during the rains on wild creepers, has a strong smell and is almost equal in the size to a ping pong ball. The poachers pluck the fruits and carefully open them with the help of a knife. They then place fishing hooks inside them. The end of the hook is tied to a small string that is about two and half feet long. At the other end of this string, a small nail is tied. Once it is done, the fruits are scattered at places frequented by the antelopes.

When the herds of antelopes congregate at such places, they are tempted by their favourite fruit. And as they swallow the deadly bait, the hook gets painfully stuck inside their mouth or, still worse, in their throat. The choking gives way to agonising madness while the string attached to the fishing hook hangs down from their mouth with a savage nail at its end. The unfortunate buck discovers the irritant hanging down from his mouth. Thinking that it is the cause of pain in his mouth or throat he desperately tries to get rid of it. The ungulates normally use their hind leg for such purposes and as he hits the strings to pull the irritant out, it usually gets stuck in the space between the hooves. The pointed nail also catches the leg and the harder the kick, the deeper the hook gets buried into the jaw or throat. This renders the poor animal completely incapable of any action. He finally falls down on the ground in a ungainly position with his hind leg tied to his mouth.

The hidden hunters watch the struggling animals from a distance and as soon as a few of the bucks are grounded, they rush up to them and finish the task.

Another animal high on the shopping list of poachers is the great Indian elephant. The north eastern parts of the country are known to harbour the largest population of these pachyderms in the entire Indian subcontinent. They are under attack for several reasons.

For instance, the official reports proclaim that the shrinking Meghalaya forests can now support only 700 elephants but the state has over 2,500 elephants. Although there are an estimated 23,000 elephants in the country, their habitat has been severely fragmented much because of the slash and burn cultivation followed by the tribals. Once deprived of their fodder, the elephants turn to raiding the crops growing on the land which was previously their favourite habitat. This gives the poachers a good opportunity to strike upon the massive animals more vehemently. They kill them in the fields and even trail them deep into the jungle, using various devices to accomplish their purpose.

The indigenous inhabitants of Assam, namely Garo, Mompa, Bodo and Duffla tribals are noted for their elephant hunting skills. Centuries of their association with the jungle and its life has gifted them with a profound knowledge of animals and their ways. In the process, they have successfully invented several methods to claim them.

In the first method, the poachers use a heavy iron block roughly weighing four or five *maunds* (about 200 kg). One end of the block is tied with a massive thick rope while on the opposite end that faces towards the ground, pointed nails of eight to ten inches length are carved out on it. This block is

then hung from a big and stout tree with the help of the thick rope over the path usually taken by the elephants. The rope is strung through five or six metal rings which are kept in place with the help of short wooden pegs fixed into the ground. It requires a stupendous effort of ten to fifteen men to pull the iron block up the tree at a height of 15 to 20 feet from the ground. Then the lower end of the rope is tied between two trees across the path of the elephant, normally four feet above the ground. The hunters then conceal themselves in the jungle and wait for the elephants.

When the passing elephant hits the rope, he perceives it as a wine or creeper, and continues to advance in his pursued direction. He drags the rope with him and as it tightens with the pull, the holding rings are released from the rope as well as the supporting pegs. This gives a sudden release to the rope which slithers up, and the deadly iron block comes down. It falls on the head or the back of the animal and causes him great mortal injury. The severity of the blow may either knock him unconscious or break his spinal cord, or may make him incapable of any movement. The hunters then arrive and with all the time in the world at their disposal, they slaughter him with swords, spears, axes and other primitive weapons.

Elephants have a very stubborn retentive vitality of life. They cannot be killed instantly, so they are slowly hacked to pieces while still alive.

In south India, tusker elephants have been facing a serious threat from poachers, over the last decade in Orissa, Andhra Pradesh and Tamil Nadu. Elephant ivory is precious material. In the language of poachers, it is white gold. In smuggling markets, the high price it fetches is valuable inducement to the poachers. Modern high velocity rifles and blinding flash lights have made their destruction a relatively simple affair. But still, in remote areas of these states, many poaching gangs operate to massacre these beasts with the poisoned arrows and spears. The poison put in use is prepared from the leaves of a herb called *sidjuha* in Ayurveda. It is abundantly available in the forests and its leaves are plucked from the plants in a large quantity. Then in a big vessel, which is half full of water they are put to boil. The fire is kept burning for seven to eight days to continue the boiling. Meanwhile, the weaned out leaves are continuously removed and fresh ones are continuously added in the pot. The poison keeps on boiling on a slow fire and at the end, a thick, viscous substance is left at the bottom of the vessel. This decoction is not poisonous by itself but when it mixes with the blood it reacts rapidly to the fatal extremities.

The tribals have a very queer procedure to examining the killing potential of this poison. A man slashes a knife wound on the upper portion of his arm and allows his blood to trickle down up to the fingertips of that hand. This forms a long rill of blood on his hand. Then the poison dipped arrow is brought in contact with the blood at the fingertip of the man. With the consequent chemical reaction, the crimson of blood starts turning blackish. The blood flow of the arm is naturally downward, but the efficacy of the poison, when now turns it blackish, moves upward. The speed with which it moves upward, shows the power of how quickly it will effect the quarry. As soon as it nears the wound, the observer neatly wipes it off with water and a herbal antidote. If the poison climbs up slowly, then the thick decoction is boiled again into an even thicker consistency to make it more effective.

The special arrows used to dip into this poison have six to eight inch long pointed iron tips, fixed firmly upon them. These iron tips or shafts once coated with poison are dried in the sun. Later on, four to six layers of poison are coated on the shafts, transforming the arrows into a genuine sucker of life. As soon as the arrow strikes the victim, the wooden shaft joined by wax falls on the ground and the pointed tip of steel pierces deep into the body of the animal and there it remains stuck for good. Normally within ten minutes after the attack, the animal becomes unconscious and according to its capacity of resistance against the effect of poison he may take two to ten hours to die. If the poison is weak and slow, then the elephant may not eventually die, but he will inevitably suffer from its effect and become permanently crippled. This will eventually lead him to a horrible death by hunger and thirst, when he is absolutely helpless to protect itself from predators and scavengers of the jungle who may mercilessly feed on his motionless body before he is dead.

In traditional Indian medicinal lore, a long list of medicines is prepared from various part of bodies of animals. As a result, a fair number of wild creatures are sacrificed and those who are in great demand are killed as soon as they are seen. The obsession for aphrodisiacs, has spread like an epidemic and the animals are paying a price for it. There are over 50 such unfortunate creatures who are mercilessly slain for lecherous men who have spent a long life of indulgence and have reached the stage where they can no longer do so. The problem may not be physical at all, but they are advised by the so-called sex specialists not to lose heart as long as the flesh of a black-faced gray *langoor* is available. This monkey tops the list of unfortunate animals. Throughout central and south India, marauding bands of poachers called Bander-walas, are always after their flesh. They are a nomadic tribe that has for centuries survived on the meat and bones of monkey. Since ages, the primitive *Birhar* tribals of Bihar have been traditional monkey hunters. Various relief and welfare scheme of successive governments have undoubtedly improved their living condition, but paradoxically, they still indulge in slaughtering monkeys under the pretext of preserving their core tribal custom. With the passage of time and the allure of market, this so called ethnic activity has become purely commercialised. Although the law strictly prohibits the killing of this animal, as it is fast disappearing since his flesh is considered a delicacy amongst natives, the nomads go to any extent, without any apparent problem to procure it.

The slender loris is yet another creature that pays a high price to prepare a medicine to cure poor men of impotence. It is an elegant, pretty little monkey. It has no tail at all, his two eyes are large, limpid brown and in spotlight, they shine beautifully like an emerald fire. This poor creature being slow in his moves is easily captured by the poachers. It is with a belief that his emerald eyes possess all the ingredients of a marvellous aphrodisiac that these animals are captured alive and the eyes are taken out from the live specimens. The poachers tear out his eyes from their sockets with a sharp knife—and he is thrown aside, to fend for himself. His life is spared because his flesh is of no use to poachers. He suffers a lingering pain and unable to support itself, he eventually dies of starvation.

The flesh of the Indian fruit bat, which is commonly referred to as flying fox, is reputed to be an effective remedy for asthma. They have been killed in such a great number that now the species is closing in towards extinction. Besides shooting and netting, the most popular method to catch them is with the use of the rosin gum. Rosin is the gum of fir trees and is very thick and sticky. Once it adheres to anything it is difficult to take it off. The poachers paste a thick viscous layer of rosin at the top of a bamboo pole covering more than two feet of its length at the other end. Then, several wild, small, strong smelling fruits are stuck upon the paster. The poachers go out in search of bats, with their bamboo poles. As they find them hanging upside down on some trees, they lift the pole and move it closer to the bats. The sight and smell of the fruit tempts the bat who leaves his perch and comes to eat the fruit. As he settles on the rosin coated part, he gets firmly stuck to it.

The poachers then lower down the bamboo pole and put him out of his misery.

This aphrodiasic-mania, has caused tremendous damage to the rhinos of Assam who have already been exploited by the poachers. In the beginning of the century, senseless slaughter by poachers and hunters combined to procure the rhino's horn, considered an effective aphrodiasic, had decimated the population to less than a dozen. In 1916, notice was taken of this alarming situation and Kaziranga was declared a sanctuary with the primary objective of preserving the rhinoceros. Since then, the scabrous biosphere reserve has heralded a commendable progress in achieving its objective.

In the beginning of the last decade, their population was reported as exceeding 1400. Out of them 1,130 lived in Kaziranga National Park, approximately 100 in Mayank Pavitra, 80 in Shorang reserve and 20 in Manas National Park. However, the last report published by the environment ministry of Assam says that rhino hunting continues on an extensive sale. It gave the details of hunting operations and the way in which they were supposed to have been conducted by the poachers. It is still not fully appreciated that in spite of burning the grass in the month of February, it again grows very fast and attains a height of 9 to 10 feet at places. It grows so densely that over great stretches of marshy land, it assumes the form of a thick mass, and becomes completely impenetrable by human standards. The rhinos are great wanderers, they move through the grass over and over again, leaving innumerable tracks as they flatten the grass and make tunnels in their way. It is on these tracks that the poachers dig their pits, camouflage them with dry twigs, branches and grass. The heavy rhinos fall into them, the poachers come and execute them to cut away their precious horns.

As if to tag the fate of rhinos with the poacher's luck, nature has cared to make rhinos the creatures of habits. One of their settled tendencies is to pile up their dung heaps at one spot. They always prefer to come back to a particular place to empty their bowels. Poachers simply discover a rhino dung heap and, concealed in a nearby place, wait there. Avid animal-watchers claim that wherever a rhino may be wandering, at the time of bowel pressure he will not relieve himself there and not hesitate to cover a great distance to come back to his self-created favourite heap. Needless to say, as he comes the poachers take care of him.

The report also counted the yearwise number of the rhinos killed by poachers. A brief mention of the figures will reveal how the conservation efforts have suffered a severe setback against the ravages of poachers. As the proclamations go, 25 rhinos were killed in 1981, 22 in 1982, 44 in 1983, 30 in 1984, 12 in 1985, 13 in 1986, 28 in 1987, 16 in 1988, 15 in 1989 and 48 in 1990. Up to the June 1991, six rhinos had already been shot. However, it is important to notice that the Forest Department does not claim any substantial increase in the rhino population. It has remained around 1100 for last many years. It shows that the multiplication which by standards should be 100 plus each year only supplements the loss of poaching. Thus the killing rate is much higher than said. A rough guess shows that around 1000 rhinos have been killed in last 10 years. It is largely surmised that this hunting had been accomplished by tribal hunters just across the border who infiltrate into India from the regions of Burma and China.

Dr. Desmond Bradley Martin of I.U.C.N. conducted a survey on rhinos, sponsored by World Wild Life Fund in India, China, Taiwan, Hongkong, North Yemen and several other Asian countries. The outcome of his result dispelled the traditionally established myth that Asian prize the rhino horn is an aphrodisiac. He found them chiefly using it as a fever reducing drug. This vital revelation may lead to a search for alternatives to the rhino horn. Dr Martin writes in I.U.C.N. Bulletin. "There is a booming market of rhino horns in North Yemen where it is used to make the handles of traditional daggers. Apparently, Yemenis returning with their savings from neighbouring Saudi Arabia are prepared to pay top prices for the real thing. This is one reason why the wholesale price of rhino horn has rocketed twenty-fold over the past five years."

For ages, the trade of the rhino horn has been done with the South East Asian and Middle East countries. Arabian Sheikhs who traditionally treated it as the strongest-ever available medicine for the purpose of sexual stimulation, required more and more horns, thus pushing up its demand in the international market. This myth has been completely scotched by scientific researches, which show that the horn contains absolutely no stimulating ingredient in it. It is an undisputed fact that this persisting belief has been vitally responsible for the mass scale extermination of this chump headed simpleton beast.

Temptation to make quick money is great amongst poachers. And the rhino horn is a sure panacea to their poverty. All they have to do is to kill a rhino, and money comes in. In 1978, the forest department of Assam had advertised an auction for a few confiscated rhino horns. The highest offer received by the auctioneers was Rs 16,000 per kg. Two years later in 1980, the auction price of the rhino horn had risen to Rs 62,500 per kg. No sale was, however, done. This pattern in the differences of the price shows that a sudden rise in poaching is also connected with the shortage of supply. The prices rise very high as the demand increased. I will not, therefore, be surprised if this sudden spurt in poaching is also connected with demand in North Yemen.

The fate of the smaller animals has proved no less harder than their bigger cousins. Snakes, lizards, rabbits, foxes, squirrels, mongoose, porcupines all have been thoughtlessly killed by the poachers. In October 1991 and then again in August

1992, the police and excise officials intercepted two trucks on the Ghaghra highway of Bahraich district in which sacks crammed with skins of snakes, lizards, rabbits and jackals were found. A few persons were arrested in this connection and the haul of the skins with other incriminating articles was confiscated from their possession. The driver and his allies were later subjected to intensive interrogation. Their startling disclosures regarding the involvement of a few influential persons of the area in this trade was unbelievable.

Though the identity of the kingpin remained a closely-guarded secret, yet whatever they narrated about their modus operandi was truly confounding.

None of the skins in the bags, the driver told the officials, was from poisonous snakes, "we don't remove the skins from poisonous snakes at all. Rather, we burn them altogether to prevent them from coming back to life and also to prevent the vengeful *naagin* (female serpent) from tracking down the killer among us." The latter part of his statement obviously refers to the myth that after a serpent is killed, its eyes retain an image of the killer and its mate, if it happens to look into the dead snake's eyes, carries that image and tracks down the killer.

"We only collect the skins of non-poisonous snakes. We are farmers and we know the importance of rat-snakes in protecting our crops from the raids of field mice. Snakes kill and eat them, yet we know that the snake skin is valuable in the market so we skin the snake alive and throw it aside," the man said casually.

The unfortunate snake may not always die in his skin-less state, as, through the process of moulting, a skin layer regenerates. Nevertheless, it is terrible to imagine the poor reptile's agony, with its exposed green and white flesh, squibbling and writhing on the ground in acute agony. On the other hand, its skin is coated with salt and copper sulphate and preserved.

Jackals, foxes and wolves are killed by the *jin* trap method. After being skinned, their bodies are left to rot and being picked clean by vultures. The bones, when left dry, are carted back to the village and sold to the men who deal in animal products.

(III)

The government's plan to provide electricity in all rural areas including the core tribal centres has paved a new way of easy poaching by electrocution. The poachers insert aluminium wires in the hollow stem of a reed grass. Having made a long chain of it they run it on the ground over the fields where the animals come to feed at night. They contact the wire with electric lines and make it live with high potential charge, ranging from 440 volts to 1000 volts. In the night, the animals venture out of the jungle and coming into contact with these wires, are electrocuted. It is largely used to kill the wild boars and through carelessness human beings also become occasional victims. Often complete sounders of pigs which carry over twenty members are practically wiped out. Their sight proves that it is not only illegal but also an unethical offence.

Not only the forests and notified reserves, but even the remote isolated pockets are not free from the curse of poaching. Almost all the rivers, lakes and ponds that fall within the jungle regions and cities are not left unsullied by these poachers.

The first kind amongst them are the petty poachers who use rods and nets to obtain their catch, whereas the second are the big businessmen who do not use these puny instruments, for with them, the work will be too hard and the catch will be too small. They work on a massive scale but do not hunt all through the month. The ideal period to kill fish starts with the arrival of moonlit nights. When the moon is luminous and nights are bright, they go to the rivers or pools in search of fish. During this time, the large fish of the river generally congregate near the banks of the river apparently to feed and sleep in the shallow waters.

The poachers arrive secretly, locate such spots and explode their home-made crude bomb into the water. They ferry in the water on a canoe, a wooden boat made out of single tree trunk. Two to three circular caracles are attached to it. They are constructed of a bamboo frame covered with buffalo hide. They sit in the canoe and gently float down the stream. They visit every pool and the respective point where the fish are concentrating. A relentless killing starts. They light the fuse and, one by one, throw the bomb into water. The explosions slaughter thousands of small fish and stun a number of larger ones. If the bomb is powerful enough then it can cover an area up to 20 or 30 sqr. yards within the water, killing all the fish that are swimming within this radius. Slowly, the casualties rise to the surface. The poachers quickly collect them with the help of the net, attached to the caracles. An avaricious loading is done till the caracles are full almost to the sinking point and then the rest of the fish, generally the smaller ones that have been killed in thousands, and are of not much edible value, are allowed to go waste. The poachers proceed to repeat their operations elsewhere, collecting only the large specimens and discarding the smaller ones that later rot and contaminate the pool or are eaten by crocodiles or other fish. Such a mass destruction of fish is a terrible wastage. It may bring

advantage to a few persons, but the country is deprived of a valuable natural resource.

In yet another method, a potion of herbal poison called 'Bangi' in South India is poured in the small water ponds. It sucks the oxygen element and within minutes the fishes come over the surface of water gasping for air. They are quickly removed and washed in fresh water otherwise they do not remain edible. Strong poison also drops birds and animals who drink water, senseless. The poachers later do away with them.

The Indian salt water crocodile is presently one of the rarest species of reptiles found in the peninsula, and till the year 1970, the rivers of Sunderbans area of Bengal harboured this species of crocodile in great abundance. The same year a civil war broke out in the neighbouring country of Bangladesh (then East Pakistan). The Pakistani army let loose a great reign of terror on the people of that country. Their atrocities led to a chain of several unfortunate circumstances, leading to a great exodus of lakhs of people into India. This country accepted them and arranged for their food, shelter and other requirements. A majority of these migrants were fishermen by profession and they were offered all the facilities by the government. Nevertheless they managed to sneak out of their camps and travelled up to the attractive forest areas of Bengal and Assam with an idea of seeking permanent settlement in India. They intended to make hunting a means of earning their livelihood. Soon they launched a merciless war against the marine wealth of the Indian peninsula killing fish, alligators, tortoise, prawns, and crocodiles. The last-named were their primary target and the gruesome methods they used to kill them can cause indignation in every sportsman.

In their novel method, the poachers take a skin of a lamb or kid and its discarded entrails, *viz* stomach and intestine etc.

The offals are emptied and the waste is replaced by a few kilograms of quick lime. Once tightly filled, they are placed inside the skin of the lamb. The folds are neatly stitched to prevent their charge from falling out. The dummy lamb is made to stand erect on four wooden legs, and is kept on the banks of the river infested with crocodiles. The rising smell of the offals coming out of the dummy lamb pervades in the atmosphere and attracts crocodiles. To make doubly sure of an early kill, the poachers also carry along a live goat with them. They sit in a suitable concealment and at a short intervals they keep twisting the ears of the goat so that it bleats freely. The crocodile mistakes it with bleating of a lamb and comes over the surface of the water where the permeating smell of flesh strongly attracts him and he moves ahead to collect his dinner. The dummy is skilfully placed, partially submerged in the water to lure the crock offering him a convenient ambush. He drags it into the water, swallows it in one gulp and dives back into the river. Within a short time the trouble starts. As soon as the water is absorbed by the flakes of dry lime, its effervescence begins to rage in crocodiles stomach. The burning heat gets stronger and stronger, causing a terrible pain and restlessness to the poor creature. The crocodile in a vain attempt to overcome the agony, begins to drink more and more water which only helps to aggravate the effervescence, until his stomach becomes thoroughly bloated and bursts with a sound that resembles a mild explosion.

The unfortunate reptile dies a torturous death. Its grosteque remains come floating over the surface of the river. They bear an abhorring testimony of man's extremely sadistic enjoyment, with its intestine's protruding out of the carcass and flakes of lime still boiling into them. The wild and thoughtless onslaughts of these refugees have denuded practically all the rivers of Bengal, Assam, U.P. and Bihar of their precious wealth of crocks and alligators. In fact, no track is left of turtles in Gomti, Ghaghra, Ganga, Sharda and Yamuna rivers of U.P.

and Bihar and even the water snakes have disappeared from them.

The poaching racket is highly organised and complicated, and that is why despite severe government restrictions, it continues to flourish unabated. In the Indian metropolitan cities of Delhi, Bombay, Calcutta and Madras, the customers are enticed to the market with a wide range of choice of animal products. In Trivandrum and Coimbatore, if one has the right connection, he can procure a grand pair of elephant tusks and in the busy market of Srinagar in Kashmir, you can get any fur, skin, horn, bone or any other animal product you want. Just name it and there are a number of people who are willing to take you to the right person for a price.

The extensive poaching has resulted in the depletion of various endangered species. It has also seriously affected the genetic balance. In the government, there seems a lack of political will to implement the uniform and concrete programme for the protection of wild life. For example, the state of Jammu and Kashmir, using its special status under article 370 of the Constitution, has enacted a wildlife law that has made a complete mockery of Indian Wild Life Act. In a live example of this untidy state of affairs, the penalty for illegal trade in furs and skins of endangered species in Kashmir attracts only a nominal fine, which is normally less than one thousand rupees, roughly about 25 American dollars, whereas in the rest of India, the same offence may lead to ten year's rigorous imprisonment and may also invite dismissal from one's job, attachment of immobile property with a substantial fine and confiscation of fire-arms.

And when the Central Government took serious note of it and requested the state to amend the law to make it stricter, the state agreed but the Chief Minister, in sympathy with the fur traders, pleaded that they should be given enough time to liquidate their existing stock. The result of this ambivalence was most unexpected. The traders declared a mind-boggling stock of 1.8 lakh jackal skins, 85,000 red fox skin and 20,000 various types of furs that largely included skins of tigers, leopards, bears and deer etc. The officials concerned who had received the declaration were horrified. One of them remarked, "It is more than the total population of wildlife in the country." And I am surprised that the statement was not far from the truth.

If we go through the chain of this commercial scenario, we discover it to be solely centered around a few individuals who are called furriers by the surveillance agencies of the government. This notorious gang is found ultimately responsible for the rapid disappearance of animals. Such men operate at two different ends and reap a handsome harvest on both of them. Their strong network of agents is spread all over the forest areas of our country. They work clandestinely, encouraging hunters to kill more and more animals. Most often the uneducated and ignorant natives who are utilised to commit the actual crime by the furriers are absolutely unaware of the damage they cause to nature and their environment. They just do not know the value of the skin they are collecting by hunting. The agents purchase the hides from the natives at throw away prices and transport them to the metropolitan cities where they are cured, processed and then supplied to the manufacturers. Purses, gloves, collars of woolen coats, caps etc. are made from them and find their way into the market where they are sold at exorbitant prices.

Then comes the second end of the chain. It comprises the customers who, in order to satisfy their vanity or gratify their craving for beautiful things, unscrupulously encourage the trade.

In the fashionable market of Europe, a leopard skin coat sells at a price which is equivalent to four lakh rupees in Indian currency. And the precondition is that the skin should be undamaged. If the animal is hunted in a clumsy way, his skin may necessarily bear the mark of several injuries, inflicted by bullets, swords, arrows and spears. These result in large perforations, scratches and even gaping holes, and thus spoil the quality of the skin, at times rendering it completely useless for the fur trade. It is not possible to make coats, jackets and chesters from such skins. The patchwork to match rosettes, howsoever, finely and dextrously done, is difficult and the original tinge of the skin is almost never revived. So, in order to keep their skins perfectly unscratched, the tigers and leopards are caught by trapping, netting and caging methods. They are drugged and hanged, and often red hot iron rods are pushed through their rectum to kill them. The accent on killing leopards is so great that their numbers have dwindled rapidly, bringing the animal on the verge of extinction. The international gangs of smugglers who trade in animal products also bear the responsibility of their transportation. They have their own business morals. The items, after full payment for them is made, are left in the shop with an address where the customer wants them to reach. The agents warranty the customer with a safe delivery of goods and in turn, the latter has to pay an additional 15 per cent of the total cost.

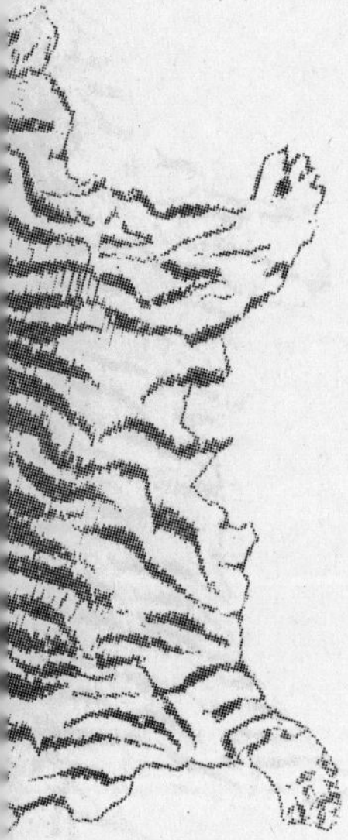

While the poachers are getting more organised, the forest patrol continues to remain badly equipped and short of staff to counter this growing threat. For instance, in my province of Uttar Pradesh, the total forest area is estimated to cover 55,000 sq. km. and there are less than 500 wildlife guards who are assigned with the job of patrolling this area. This means that each guard has to cover a beat of roughly 100 sq. km. whereas under the prescribed norms of the Central Government, one guard is required for every 10 sq. km. With these anomalies, the forest authorities are left with no option but to maintain silence over the poaching activities or even better, they connive with the poachers and receive succulent gifts in return. At times, some odd representative of law who has the desire to do something constructive, tries to save the situation from further degeneration. Not bothered about the consequences, he raids the hide-outs of poachers, confiscates some skins and other incriminating material, and even gets a few poachers imprisoned. The undaunted officer, despite his valiant efforts, is never able to punish that notorious individual who is in the pivot of all this. This man always has a safe line of retreat and he successfully escapes from the tentacles of law. Thereafter, commences the grind of detailed investigations; the achievement is highlighted in the press with headlines screaming as "Poaching racket busted." "The big kill", "Big seizure of skins", "The cruel business of poaching" and so on, giving an assurance to the people about the renewed efforts of the government to curb poaching. Finally, reports are prepared and the great haul is locked in a godown. Then the poachers again become active, for they know that there are some sympathisers in the forest department on whom they can always rely. Then one fine morning a few selected skins, or at times the complete stock, mysteriously disappears from the lock-up. To cover this up, the administrator immediately draft a report on this issue. It generally states that as the skins were seriously infected by pests, they were written off and burnt to ashes. All the requirements of the law are thus formally satisfied and the file is closed.

Now the question arises that for how long will we allow this brutal business to continue and how long will the precious heritage of our country be swindled and robbed by unscruplous elements? Actually, conservation of wildlife depends largely on a radical change in our attitudes. The days of hunters in India are practically over, yet sadly, there are a few trigger-happy ones who do not seem inclined to accept this fact and continue their ravages on our dwindling fauna. In such conditions, hunting has ceased to be a sport, it has become a crime of the first order. Human population explosion and the growing demand for food has invaded and eroded the jungles. Millions of hectares of land which once belonged to animals has yielded way to farmers and town planners. The developmental programmes have converted many jungles into flourishing trade centres. The contrasts are startling, in many remote townships, tigers and other wild animals roam just behind eating houses and movie theatres. Shopping complexes have come up at places which were once exclusive preserves of the tough denizens of the dark. For example, in Palia Kalan of Lakhimpur district near Dudhwa forest, a tiger was found comforting itself beneath a small kiosk of a cigarette-*paan* seller. In neighbouring Sampoorna Nagar, a man-eating tiger made a kill just behind a travelling theatre one evening, and all the while the show was going on. Recent examples of this unhealthy encroachment are the deaths of tigers and other wild animals getting run over by trains as it has happened in Mala and Dudhwa forest blocks of Pilibhit and Lakhimpur districts.

Poaching has assumed pernicious proportions. It has drastically influenced the multiplication of gene pools which is a grim augury for the future. The latest investigations show that amongst malar animals approximately 400 Tigers, 200 Elephants, 300 Leopards and over a 100 Rhinos are killed every year. If it continues then the successive generations may not hear the mighty roar of a tiger which travels over the mountains and the valleys, rumbling like thundrous clouds; or the leopards loitering casually near the villages in search of a quick, stealthy meal, or marvel at the sight of bison herds browsing and scanning the horizons across the vast grasslands, or shudder at the trumpet blast of exhilaration emanating from tusker bulls that lead the elephant herds.

How then life would lack the liveliness and diversity in absence of multifarious beauties of wildlife! Only dogs, kites, rats, crow and domestic cats would survive because of their innate conduciveness to co-exist with human beings and adjust to the dynamically transformed patterns of life. Above all, because they are not edible fare.

The process of evolution and civilisation has put man in

total control of the destiny of the planet earth. But that does not mean that anything which is not of obvious use to humans, but has nevertheless been surviving in its own niche, should be eliminated from the scheme of things as seen through population, such as housing, industry or farming, must take into account the interest of the original inhabitants of land—the wild animals.

All animals occupy a specific place in the eternal ecological chain. Even if an animal is of no use to us, it plays its predestined part in this chain. Being in a position to alter this chain, we have no right to displace, or worse, remove any link from it. We have our own kind, for the sake of this planet, our civilisation and above all, the process of evolution which never slows down or stops.

6
The Sugarcane Tiger

Beer Singh, a Sikh farmer in Parsaiya village, was ploughing his field with a harrow attached to his tractor. It was early morning and while he negotiated a turn close to a patch of sugarcane, he saw a tigress leisurely emerge out of it at the far end of the field. A pair of cubs trailed behind her. At the sight of the tractor, the mother tigress stopped in her tracks, but the little furry balls took a fancy to the foreign object and turned playful. They were completely unafraid of its awkward sounds. Cantering gingerly, they came near the machine. At first they ran along with it and then began to bound around it. This was something unexpected as, considering the loud, sputtering sounds of the tractor engine, even domesticated animals who are supposed to be familiar with such sounds, felt disturbed and always moved away from the source of the sound. There was no reason why tigers should also not do the same, thought the farmer. But the scene being enacted here was different from what he thought. The man was mortally terrified and he did not dare to stop the tractor or accelerate the speed in order to run away.

The farmer mastered his urge to flee with great difficulty. He tried to maintain his calm, though his heart beat heavily and profuse sweat rills coated his body. Mumbling supplications, he continued to drive his tractor at uniform speed.

Running around a moving tractor apparently did not turn out to be all that enjoyable for the small creatures so they abandoned this play and then embarked on a new adventure. They started jumping over the spinning harrow disc to have their thrills. While all this was going on, the mother arrived near the field. She sat down on the elevated edge and curiously watched the cubs performing the trick with dexterity, that showed their natural and inherited proficiency in mastering difficult manoeuvres. For the Sikh, this was an extremely dangerous situation. A little misjudgement on the part of the cubs could make them fall on the sharp-edged discs of the harrow and get injured seriously, even fatally. This would undoubtedly initiate the tigress into action and the farmer found himself reluctant to imagine the dreadful consequences. He continued to plough his field and in the process, suffered a most severe experience of his life, painfully conscious of any eventuality that could set in any moment.

The bizarre drama continued for more than half an hour then suddenly the mother stood up, released the monosyllabic sounds of a--oo-m, a--oo-m twice, followed by a long drawn cough to call her cubs. Having done this, she entered the same thicket of sugarcane out of which she had emerged. The low, moaning calls instantly alerted the cubs and they suddenly seemed to have lost all interest in their game. They left the tractor and running after each other, followed their mother to disappear from the scene.

The scene enacted on that fine morning was not an isolated one. In varying degrees, such events keep occurring every now and then in the whole Terai area of Uttar Pradesh and lately it has acquired magnified proportions.

Why has it suddenly increased ? To answer this question, we must at first briefly analyse the crucial factor of biotic disturbances which have taken a gigantic toll in most of the forest areas.

To start with, the environment of Terai is composed of three different elements—the Sal forest, the grasslands and the riverine forest. The Sal is a straight trunk, hardwood and gregarious tree which averages 100 feet in height. A great number of trees, creepers, grasses, herbs and ferns grow along with or under the Sal. The annual grass burning that is done to perpetuate the grasslands and discourage the trees from moving in perhaps emboldens the predominance of this fire-resistant tree. The tree is of the deciduous category but it never grows completely leafless and with the arrival of the spring season, it blossoms with mildly scented creamy white flowers.

The second element is the alluvial marshy plains. Though a few patches of such terrain interspersed with Sal forest still survive in the enclosure which is now compartmentalised as the Dudhwa National Park within the greater Terai area, the tall, dense strands of the ikra grass that just 40 years back stretched for massive distances along the copious water course of the Sharda river, have now completely disappeared. It was a great virgin habitat of wild animals and old-timers recall that the grassland which appeared a monotonous green mass, actually contained a great diversity of vegetation. The variety of grass species in it were no less than 50 in number.

The third element is the riverine forest, which is an interesting mixture of Sal and grass forest. It dominates along the water courses and supports a dense undergrowth.

This magnificent scabrous region had been a traditional stronghold of the tiger population. Historically speaking, these grasslands provided the tigers with the most suitable breeding ground. The thick undergrowth and long stems of grass provided them with adequate shade and the marshy soil took care of the need for coolness of this ever-panting, heat-intolerant predator. In such an ideal and primal habitat, the rate of reproduction of tigers remained consistently high. That is why in the great old days of shooting, sportsmen regarded this area as an inexhaustible supply ground of predatory population, though the tigers were subsequently destroyed at an unprecedented rate. The old Indian sporting literature maintains that as soon as a tiger was shot dead, his place was taken up by a new entrant to the community. The supply was constantly maintained.

But alas! these lands of pristine freshness were not allowed to last longer. The dawn of India's freedom was accompanied by the painful bane of partition. Hordes of Sikh refugees displaced from Pakistan arrived in India and the Terai area was marked as an ideal ground for their rehabilitation. The great forests and grasslands of Kheri which for centuries had been the traditional breeding grounds of tigers succumbed to the ploughers and harvesters. Hundreds of miles of land was plundered for timber, the indiscriminate felling by far served as the greatest threat to tiger survival. The erosion of their habitat was so relentless that very soon there was virtually no place left for the tigers which was not infiltrated and influenced by the neo-colonisers. The tiger had no place to migrate so they continued to stay in the area because the great cats have a strong attachment to their ranges. Even if strong odds are against them, they try to stay put in their territory. Secondly, fortunately there were still a few fragmented segments within the farmland area that could offer a nominal shelter to the harassed felines.

With an increasing difficulty, the tigers adapted themselves to the rapidly changing situation and managed to survive amid the unfriendly environs. As the biotic pressure increased, hordes of labourers arrived to seek employment in the newly-established farms. They erected their temporary shelter on the jungle land and also used it for their subsistence. These settlements of various human inhabitants posed another problems of cattle grazing. This unwarranted intrusion and its resultant hazards only helped accelerate the pace of damage. It dispersed the wild ungulates and exposed them to several cattle-borne diseases. Whereas the cattle could be treated by the veterinary people, there was no treatment for the wild animals. Even if affected by a mortal disease they preferred to maintain a safe distance from human beings, and die an inevitable death in isolation, which has ironically ordained to them by the progress of the human civilisation.

Uncontrolled fire hazards remained another deterrent to the

proliferation of wildlife. Fires disrupted the activities of mammals. During their breeding times, it destroyed a great number of the avian population which takes to nesting from March onwards and finally degraded the habitat. I believe that in majority of cases, human infiltrators are responsible for this phenomenon, who spend their time in the jungle to conduct various illegal activities such as cutting firewood, collecting honey and poaching. They often carelessly handle fire while cooking food or lighting cigarettes. Such small sparks often culminate into a roaring inferno. Natural forest fires also occur, but it is an extremely rare phenomenon and now when forest management has become a thoroughly scientific exercise, it has become an impossibility. Fire now, is rather a tool in the hands of forest management people, who intelligently use it against the deterioration of environment.

The tigers, faced also with destructive, though legitimate, shooting which was mostly organised by professionals and the indiscriminate ravages of poaching which added to their problems. It was extremely different for a tiger to find a habitat that suited all his requirements. They travelled long distances in search of a decent niche, which as a matter of fact, now existed nowhere. And finally, circumstances forced him to seek refuge in the extensive sugarcane crop adjoining the forests. In all likelihood, tigers took the tall and dense sugarcane as a replacement for the tall reed grass and thus they considered it as a natural extension of their habitat. They adapted themselves to the seasonally fluctuating heights of sugarcane strands and stayed there, feeling relatively undisturbed until the start of harvest. Though the crops were grown and manned by humans, yet this exercise did not seem to create any significant sound or disturbance.

There exists almost no buffer zone between the jungle and the cultivation fields except for the few ranges of the Dudhwa National Park. In the rest of the Terai, humans and animals freely infiltrate into each other's zone. The unimaginative planners who had allowed the immense deforestation of this area had probably never realised the necessity of creating such a buffer zone, whereas it is an indispensable part of the atmosphere which essentially maintains the ecological integrity of a natural complex. Thus, with this, there was created an extremely unpleasant situation of conflict between man and beast.

Sugarcane tiger was a new and unique fall-out of the myopic planning of massive deforestation and expansion of the highly commercialised industry of sugarcane. As a matter of fact, it is now flourishing on the land that belonged to this tribe only a few decades ago.

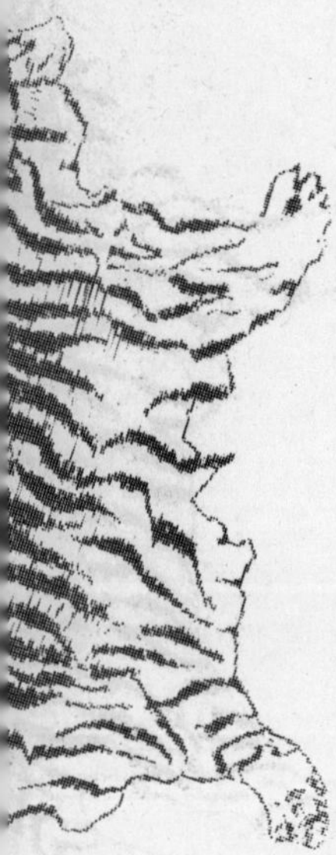

It is regrettable, that despite the constant warnings of environmentalists and ecologists, who predict dangerous consequences for life if the forest area is reduced to less than 30 per cent of the total land area, timber felling by organised poaching gangs continues unabated. In my own district of Lakhimpur Kheri, several timber gangs are operating under political patronage and practice this trade in a highly organised manner. The district is popularly mistaken as comprising immense expanses of dense forest but the bitter fact is that forests constitute only 19 per cent of its total land area.

The jungles of Dudhwa National Park with their outstretching boundary of the tiger reserve are actually smaller than their defined boundary. The park's Kishanpur and trans-Sharda ranges roughly cover 700 sq. km. area, whereas roughly 200 sq. km. of border area does not contain regular forests. A number of reasonably fragmented blocks which are shown in the government map of reserve forest, have been actually cleared and converted into prosperous farmland. It does not incorporate the sugarcane fields illegally ploughed by farmers and land-grabbers.

As per government policy of fetching more revenue, a vast

area of forest land is also given on annual contract to peasantry for cultivation. Such land, where a buffer zone can be created by extensive tree plantation, is thoughtlessly leased out to farmers. The crops grown there are always exposed to the plundering pillage of wild ungulates. The farmers spend a lot of time to protect it from them, and pass several sleepless nights, shouting clamorously and constantly beating tincans to drive away the marauders.

The practice of land leasing may lead to a fractional hike in government revenue and may also provide a scanty subsistence to a needy populace, but it certainly does not support the principle of conservation. Here lies the contradiction which concerns the developmental progress and the vital need to conserve environment. The need to strike a balance between the two is recognised, and it is for the planners to find out how best to accomplish it. Government funds have been, and are being, spent on apparently non-productive counts like popularisation of our ethnic diversity abroad, whereas the very indigenous and irretrievable natural diversity is allowed to decimate. A more contrasting example will be difficult to find than the case of a street-smart animal-trainer who is flown at great government expense to show his pet bear or monkey perform in front of appreciative western audiences, but is allowed to lead an aimless, poverty-stricken life in a slum back home.

Not to digress from the subject, it is worthwhile to know that by international standards, the Dudhwa National Park is quite small, even though it is considered quite large by Indian, or even south Asian standards. Both the south and north blocks of the Dudhwa Park are completely independent and work as a compact environment by themselves. The authorities also claim to take every precaution to minimise disruption of the biosphere and maintain a balance between nature and man. If we accept these claims on face value, the park does have its limitations. Considering the average tiger population, which is counted and maintained as exceeding 90 by the park authorities, it is questionable to accept it. We cannot ignore the fact about the park's capacity to contain this tiger population. The experts appear scarcely conscious of this reality about how this gargantuan population will adjust itself within the limited territory of 900 or 700-odd sq. km. of mixed forest land.

Coming to the nature of tigers, they are solitary and strictly territorial animals. No less then 35 sq. km. area is required by a single male tiger to ramble in freedom. They do not tolerate any interference by the members of their own kind and in the territory of a strong tiger, no vagrant male is welcomed on a permanent basis. Normally, one and often two to three females share a male tiger's territory and generally there is an easy compatible relationship. But a sizeable tiger population is claimed to be there in the park, whereas in the existing condition, it cannot afford to adjust more than 40 tigers in a comfortable way. This number should be taken as a practical ceiling imposed by nature itself as, once it is crossed, the environment will start to suffer. This itself gives a natural answer to the problem of sugarcane tiger. The jungles are already full and no room is left for the weaker feline. In the conflict of territory they are driven out by their stronger brothers and when they came out in the open then it is the luxuriant sugarcane crop that welcomes them offering an adequate shelter and a suitable habitat to survive.

Tigers seem to have opted for this refuge for various reasons. Firstly, the strands of sugarcane crops match with the exact characteristics of the *narkul* or the reed grass strands. The thick growth of vegetation at all the levels, and the flowering fronds at the top of the crops prevent the direct penetration of sunlight within its environment. The interior remains cool and damp. A hazy twilight permeates within, which has an extremely soothing effect on the eyes of nocturnal animals like tiger.

Secondly, the tiger displays a great intolerance to heat. He is a thirsty animal. In the heat of the day, he pants heavily with a lolling and dripping tongue. He seeks cool and shady covers or a water pond to retire at comfort. In the blistering summer, water pools in the jungle normally dry out quickly. A few survive but they also become scanty and distant. On the other hand, throughout the scorching summer months, the cane crops are profusely irrigated by artificial means. The dampness of soil and a thin film of water that floats over it provides him an ideal home.

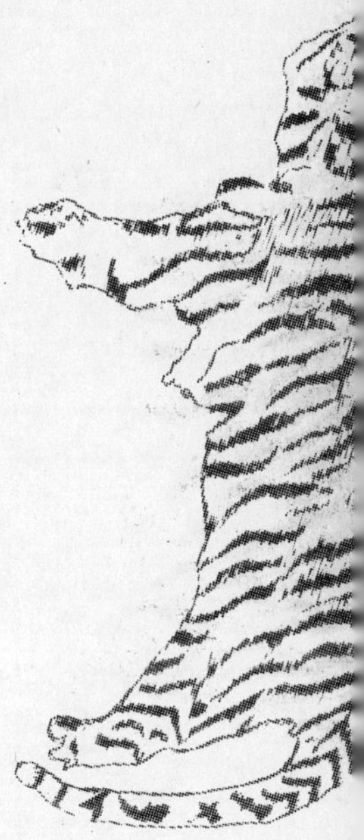

Essentially being a flesh-eater, the tiger's face, nails and body have small particles of flesh, bones and blood adhered to them. These smell, chard and attract the blue-bottle flies, which are a constant sources of irritation to the tiger. And this is the third reason for the tiger's preference for sugarcane. The thickness of crop and bad light conditions discourage the flies from entering into it and here the tigers are mercifully free from this menace.

It is said that in the forest of peninsular India, there is no definite or a well-demarcated season for courtship of a big cat but in the Terai region, tigers seem to mate after the rains and a majority of the young ones are born between February and May. The cubs, may be born in any month of the year. To give birth to her young ones, the tigress naturally searches for a dense patch of cover. This nursery should always be well concealed and should essentially have a dark interior. The spot should also be located at a position from where it can be readily defended. These preconditions are instinctively sought by the mother tigress, for the tiger cubs are born blind and helpless. They are highly vulnerable to predation by scavangers such as wolves, hyenas, jackals and foxes. Even wild boars are known to destroy and eat them. The responsibility of cub-rearing chiefly falls upon the mother, for the male tiger as a rule deserts his mate in the middle of the gestation period. This is explained by the sexual inactivity which normally sets in the tigress within a month of conception. We know that from February to May, sugarcane crops are at their best and provide the mother with a perfect hide-out to breed and the litter is relatively safe from the second and third order predators of nature.

The newly-born ones constantly demand the attention of their mother. In their thin weak voice, they are ever yelling and screaming and whenever for a short period they are left alone by their mother, they cry at their loudest and at times, crawling on their four paws, they stray away from the nursery. They thus advertise their presence to the predators. The tigress thus has to guard them consistently and meet their insistent demands. This responsibility does not let her venture out for long distances. However, hunger compels her to go out in search of prey and yet she cannot stay away for a long time bound by her motherly sentiments. If, by chance, she succeeds in procuring a kill, then it is all right but if she fails to do so for quite a few days at a stretch or finds it difficult to subdue enough prey, then her physical condition deteriorates very fast. The enfeebled tigress may also fail to produce sufficient milk for her cubs. This leads to a retardation of growth among the young ones, making them more vulnerable to early death. This induces her to make a determined stalk for a definite kill and since long perambulations are time consuming, the probability of her cubs getting exposed to danger in her absence also becomes imminent.

The tigress meets her food demands through the ready availability of domestic stock of cattle and mongrel dogs, a variety of poultry, cats and goats, etc. Owing to their association with man, they freely roam about the agricultural field, and are very easy to catch since their ability of sensing objects is dulled by their domestication. In comparison to a jungle tiger under similar conditions, procuring food is not much of a problem for a sugarcane tiger, although the frequency of bagging a catch might be lower. Crops of wheat, pulses, gram and maize, also grow within a sugarcane field, and therefore herbivores of all kinds are attracted to these fields. Wild boars, porcupines, sambhar, cheetal, hog deer and swamp deer visit these fields in the night to browze, besides domestic cattle. These animals figure on the tigers' list of prey, and while in the jungle the tigers have to travel long distances to get their dinner. Here the dinner comes right into their territory, and slain with an effort which is less as compared to the labour they have to exercise in the jungle.

Moreover, in the cultivated fields, there is no competition for food. The rival beasts of prey are stationed at distances. The proximity of cattle is an ever present temptation for the tiger. It helps to localize them. An anticipation of easy prey provides them with a strong incentive to hang around or repeatedly return to the particular place or more often confine themselves to that one area.

A manifestation of this is observed in a common bond of recognition existing between them. Farm tigers are far more adaptable to the environmental changes than the jungle tigers, who are hardly pressed for space. It is proved by their fabulous admission of human zones, in spite or retaining their inherently solitary characteristics. Some experts argue it from an interesting angle that, being evidently undernourished, because the wild-ungulates do not normally loitre in human zones and man also makes conscious effort to save his cattle and poultry.

The competition for food in no less hard than anywhere, yet one or two animals may hang around but the depredating herds from the jungle only come out when the new shoots in the crop begin to sprout. These tigers are known to display an accommodating tendency. A number of adult tigers inclusive of opposite sexes are seen to mutually share a major part of each others limited islet of diurnal cover. The understanding is that excluding a core area which is the occupying tigers private domain, command zones are mixedly established. It is only when the food conditions truly deteriorate say from bad to worse, that they migrate into different fields of similar environments.

It is observed in the jungle that the dominating males often also show a little accommodating tendency. They establish a rank order with the transient tigers and in the high density area of water sources and prey, they tend to become gregarious. A magnified form of this feature was observed in Kachida Valley of Ranthambhore National Park, in a non-family group of four tigers. The association was naturally related to the improved hunting efficiency but that was an unusual case of feline behaviour. However, with respect to sugarcane tigers in three different years I have myself known of no less than three points, all of them roughly around 20 sq. km in diameter which were shared by two males and two females. I do not know about the reasons which would satisfactorily explain this common sharing of ranges. A serious research is needed to understand this phenomena in sugarcane tigers here they subsist on a degraded suboptimal environment. It is apparent that the conclusions drawn about the jungle tigers cannot be implemented in this changed atmosphere of their environmental degradation.

Incidently, in the context of the man-eating tigers in Kheri district, Yogesh and I have conducted three entirely personal investigations during June 1979, December 1982 and November 1986. In the summer of 1979, we had gone to Dudhwa just when the man-eating menance had began to originate. A majority of the cases had occurred on the fringe area and not in the heart of the jungle. Tracing the cause of this dread we began our search for the farm tigers. For here seemed the genesis of this problem. To our surprise, we counted the pug marks of no less than nine tigers in the harvested pockets of cane between the villages of Majhgai and Bela Kalan.

At this time of the year, the heat was disastrous and the burning hot wind blew regularly during the sun up hours. Only a few pockets of over-mature cane crops, were left standing in the field. The irrigation supply to them had also been stopped, and hence, it was too warm inside the cane cluster. The tigers had provisionally retired to closeby thickets of fern and *narkul* strands that grew densly packed and tall to the height of a full grown elephant, heralding a few places with scattered trees under which, where the sunrays scarcely penetrated. It was noticed that a sizeable population of hog bear also abound in this area. These animals belonging to the same genus as the cheetal generally inhabit the outskirts of forest and live a solitary way of life, which naturally makes them vulnerable to predation. In the course of our investigations we came across two hog bear remnants recently devoured by tigers. It showed that the tigers were not facing a problem getting food. These were the spots where they spent their day in cover to beat the oppressive summer heat and later prowled through the cane fields in their nocturnal journeys. As we travelled along their trail again at two places we found the signs of two pairs of cubs living with their mother. This propensity of humans despite the availability of natural food in the vicinity was undoubtedly a reason for the initiation of man-eating tendencies among the tigers and the presence of four cubs within a territory of ten sq. km. area was certainly a remarkable feature with regard to the increasing tiger population. Later in 1986 we again came across a similar situation in Bilrayan area and believed in the hypothesis propounded and established by Shri S.R. Choudhary, then one of the Project Tiger field directors and the owner of the famous pet tigress Khairi, that reproductive dynamics in farm tigers registers a high increase in comparison to jungle tigers.

Having noted two observations of the same kind we pondered over the hypothesis and found it well on its way to be concluded into a theory.

It is highly probable that prolonged proximity to a male, or an exposure to his strongly overpowering male sexual hormone or androus pheromone may make an unattached female impulsively inclined to go in for mating, thereby leading to a higher fertility and consequently population growth rate, contrary to the prevalent theory on population control as propounded by Malthus.

The substance in this conception is supported by the fact that being the largest and most powerful of flesh-eaters, tigers have no natural enemies. The top of the food chain is a lonely and comfortable niche. In sugarcane they may project an enormous potential for increase but the still more important factor is the congenial conditions for the survival of their cubs and we know that this factor is strictly controlled by the number of prey available and in human zones the condition is no doubt very critical. The survival of the cubs is also deeply affected and it appears that a majority of them do not go along with the harrased conditions, and die. But, however, we will discuss this point at some more appropriate place.

Backed by recent researches, this might be yet another factor that compels a tiger to go in for unconventional food, such as dogs, poultry and with growing courage, even human beings.

Sugarcane cultivation adjacent to forests is also dangerous for it increases the chances of a confrontation between man and animal. The tiger's association with man has not only increased but it has also brought about a change in the tiger's attitude. Man's activities have cast a profound influence on their lives, consequently the tigers have become more cunning, more individualistic and are better able to escape a threat to their lives. This familiarity with man has also developed strong sense of courage in them. In quite a few individuals of this species, the accumulated experience about man's limitations and helplessness and their success in escaping from any probable harm from man has even exaggerated their reaction against them. Their usual curiosity and basic fear of man has considerably diluted. In many areas of Terai, sugarcane tigers are known to show an indifference to human activities. They completely disregard human presence and are not affected by the lights, sounds and movements or the mechanical gadgets used in cultivation.

These tigers, at the first opportunity, exploit the sources of food supply for humans. The act inevitably lands them in competition with man. As its result, an entirely new bahavioural pattern has begun to emerge in the farm tigers. Quite a few of them are known to have opted for diurnal ramblings besides their usual nocturnal strolls. Unprovoked demonstrations are occasionally heard of. Excessive slaughter of cattle often occurs. These are a few of the negative reactions displayed by the tigers. The tigers inside the forest are naturally better off, for plenty of cover provides them enough concealment to practice their traits. They indulge in hunts all through the night and in the morning, terminate their search and stop off at one of the halting stations within their territory. They do not have a permanent residence and are rarely to be found at one place for more than a day. Actually, these marked stations only provide them with temporary resting places from where they can go out hunting the next day.

Contrary to this, the farm tigers do not get the advantage of lavish cover all around except for the sugarcane crop itself, so they occupy more or less a permanent abode. They will get on the move taking advantage of whatever cover is available but usually show a tendency to come back to a marked home. Another departure from the natural behaviour of a jungle tiger seen in its farm counterpart is the absence of any qualms whatsoever in consuming a carcass or a kill over which vultures have operated. The jungle tiger detests the musky stink of the vulture excreta and abandons such food. Such dislike is generally absent in the sugarcane tiger.

These changes have naturally evolved in the sugarcane tiger because of those circumstances which have been forced upon him. All his actions and reactions appear to be a deliberate defiance of their tribes' very own special characteristics. The prolonged comprehension of human relationship and an appreciable need for survival and adjustment inevitably brings them together to the detriment of both.

Who can appreciate the extent of the statement better than Choudhary Mahendra Pal Singh, a *jat* farmer who lives in Bujhia farm, 4 km. to the east of the township of Palia Kalan. It was a cold winter evening. Choudhary's servants had finished the work of the day. After herding all the cattle into the shed, they departed to the neighbouring village where they lived. Choudhary was tired with the arduous work of the day. He sat and relaxed in his chair, sipping a refreshing cup of hot tea. Half-lying on his chair, he switched on his transistor to listen to the AIR news bulletin. While he looked out of the window to enjoy the thickening dusk, he happened to perceive an ill defined shape entering his *verandah*. It leisurely crossed over and went towards the cattle shed. The farmer took it to be the mongrel dog which laid about his farm. But hardly a few seconds later he heard the choking and rasping sounds of his bull coming from the cattle shed. These were followed by brief sounds of struggle as if the bull was frantically trying to break the rope, around its neck in order to run away.

He cursed them loudly in anger, much in the belief that the rival bulls which did not like each other had once again locked their horns. He went out to separate them, before they got down to serious trouble. He took a torch as there was no electricity in his cattleshed. As he lit it towards the scene of the commotion, he was shocked to see his bull lying dead on the ground and just a few feet behind him, two reddish orbs gleamed brightly in the feeble glare of the torch. At first, the farmer thought these were the eyes of another of his bulls, but these eyes were extremely bright, carrying the lustre of burning fire in them. It was after a couple of minutes that Choudhary realised that what he was looking into were surprisingly the eyes of a tiger. Indeed as the tiger had sensed the arrival of a human being, he had left his grip on the bull and to further avoid the encounter with the interfering man, had retreated behind a small clump of straw and sat there in a crouching position looking into the eyes of the intruder. The farmer maintained his nerve and retreated slowly not daring to attempt to rescue the bull. He covered some 10 paces walking backwards, and taking an about turn, ran into the house. There he asked the womenfolk of the house to sit in the rooms and close the doors tightly from the inside.

Choudhary's youngest daughter, Dr. Nirmala who works as a principal in a local school, made an audacious attempt to get the gun, despite the warning of her father. She went out of her room and crossing the *verandah* and courtyard, reached the isolated hutment where the single-barrel 12-bore gun was kept. She locked the door from inside and fired four shots one after another in the air. At the same time, the yelling sounds of womenfolk also started.

This intimidated the tiger. He came out of the cattleshed, and quickly retreated to the sugarcane field. In his effort to find his way out of the house, he moved around in the premises. In this process, he paused momentarily and inspected all the flimsy doors. He sniffed them and pressed them with his forepaw, as if mentally reviewing every single detail of the crude and ineffectual defence. After sometime he finally found his way, jumped over the boundary wall to disappear into the darkness.

Nirmala grossly doubted whether all the pandemonium

could really drive away a tiger who had just made an easy kill but was deprived of it. There was no reason why he should not make another attempt to get hold of it. It was difficult to ascertain the immediate whereabouts of the tiger. She and her brother lit a fire in the middle of the courtyard and in the dead darkness of night, her mother and her sister-in-law carried a lantern and went out to the adjacent village to get some help. It was a brave act indeed. But done in excitement. Soon a posse of men arrived on the scene and, to keep the tiger at bay, a great din from all available metallic and wooden items—was created. The tiger kept hovering around the farmhouse the entire night. He even made two half-hearted attempts to reclaim the possession of his kill, then finally, shortly before dawn, as the faint streak of light had begun to show itself, he finally gave up and left for his sugarcane retreat.

It was three days later, when the same tiger struck again, four miles to the south of Choudhary's farm. In this settlement, a poor peasant called Bachchu Pasi lived with his small family in an isolated hutment. The tiger, apparently still hungry, wandered into this area and set his eyes upon Bachchu's cattle, but here, an extraordinarily interesting incident took place that turned the tables on the tiger.

Poverty-stricken Bachchu earned a meagre income from one acre of land and two milch cows, whose milk he sold to the local villagers. Just a week before this incident, a fierce and sturdy stud bull had come loitering to the area. Since it was the month of February and Bachchu's cow was in heat, the bull was taken as a welcome guest and he too settled in the area, attracted by the cows. He often courted the cows in the grazing fields, but due to his wandering nature he did not like to come into the resting ground. When the cows returned in the evening, he habitually accompanied them up to the outer fringe of the hutment but then, to spend the night at will, he himself retired to some close by fields to browse in the unguarded crops! Bachchu did not have a shed for his cattle but this lapse was compensated by a shadowy *neem* tree, which stood just a few yards behind his shanty. The ground around it served as a provisional pen with several wooden pegs fixed on it. In winter, the milkman usually covered his cattle with a canvas cloth and under the canopy of the tree, tethered them in the open.

So that very night Bachchu tied his cows in the open and went to sleep in his thatched hut. Towards midnight, the same vagrant tiger happened to pass through that way in his desultory search for prey. Sensing the presence of unbarricaded cattle, he stopped for an ambush and quickly seized a small calf that was tied close to the field. As the carnivore's fangs sought their way deep through the flesh of his prey, the calf desperately let out its last agonized bray. The sounds of death travelled in the silence of the night. They were heard by the stud bull who was habitually hanging around in a field around the hutment. He became outraged and came thundering to the spot to investigate the cause and upon discovering a tiger involved in the killing act, he instantly attacked him. The bull worked himself up into a furious anger so much so that the tiger despite his minor demonstrations, soon found it difficult to stand against formidable charge. He soon fled into the darkness. The bull too went after him to teach him a lesson. Meanwhile, the cowyard was all disturbed and its all inmates created an obnoxious din, trying to break away the ropes from the pegs. Some time later, having given a thoroughly defeating run to the tiger, the bull again returned to the shelter and with all pride stood there as guard over the dead calf.

Bachchu had awakened by now. He lay utterly benumbed and paralysed with fear, intently listening to the sounds of the duel, in a horrible expectancy that the tiger may come crashing into his humble home. Sleep did not return to his eyes for the rest of that night, although the din had long subsided. The next morning, Bachchu was greatly relieved to discover the benign gesture of the great bovine.

The rest of the day he spent in constructing a temporary shelter which he barricaded with barbed wire. But, apparently the visiting predator of the previous night had marked the spot as a definite store of beef, for that night he materialized on the scene again. The cows went wild upon sensing his presence. The tiger made persistent efforts to reach them but the barricade proved a tough obstacle. The attempts provoked the cows to cry hysterically, and in the silence of the night. They were again picked up by the stud bull. He came crashing straight to the barricade and challenged the tiger. Discretion was evidently the better part of valour for the tiger did not react to his challenging grunts and again moved away.

The next morning the tiger's pug marks around the cattleshed showed that, cautiously avoiding the bull it had remained in the area in some fervent hope. Discouraged, apparently by the security measures and the presence of a self-appointed guard in the form of the stud bull, the tiger had made no initiative for an attack. Later, the days passed off peacefully. The tiger maintained his distance and moved away for good, showing due respect for the daring bull. And Bachchu Pasi rid of the added discomfiture in his life was left free to continue his battle against poverty without a tiger's shadow.

These are the two of many examples of the tigers reduced fear of man. This outrageous boldness is a dangerous signal because, besides cattle killing, it can conveniently lead the tiger into the malicious trait or man-eating.

The menace of sugarcane tiger is a horrendous phenomenon. It cannot be taken casually. The tigers who have an excellent fitness for predatory life—a swift capture, killing and eating of living prey are decidedly dangerous animals and once accustomed to living in the fields of sugarcane, they definitely become more dangerous than their contemporaries in forests. They display every characteristic of grass tigers, who, owing to the inordinate density of grass can neither be seen before hand and, paradoxically, nor can they see well until the intruder almost bumps into it. We know that the tigers do not run down their prey. They stalk noiselessly on soft pads and thus depend more on tread than on speed and that is the indispensable elements of their hunting. Tigers are heavily armed predators of colossal strength. They exhibit ultrafast reflexes as they live in a habitat of restricted vision, where they get no time to consider their action, because anything that moves in the jungle, whether it is seen or unseen is their substantial and conquerable prey.

The tiger acts according to the dictates of its natural impulse to attack, and an unexpected meeting with man is liable to produce disastrous consequences for the latter. We must remember two things; first, that a tiger's large up standing ears are highly attuned to catch air borne sounds and in respect to these sounds his sense of direction is extraordinarily accurate and secondly, that a tiger's muffled tread and sinuous gliding movement combine to effect his stealthy approach to his prey. They are marvellously fit for striking the prey, holding and killing him immediately. They are exempted from the complications of dentition. They have scissor-like teeth and four long straight canines. Lateral motion is absent in the jaws of tiger. Their broad condyle bone is set so perfectly into its socket, that a prey's departure from up and down scissors-like action is impossible and so are his claws. They remain sheathed in his talon's and are kept sharp and safe by this peculiar arrangement. While catching the prey they suddenly project out, hold and demobilize the animal. Precisely all this arrangement ensures the greatest power of destruction and the simplest mechanism for producing it.

Given this propensity, even if he catches a human being

haphazardly, his claws and teeth strive to retain the hold on the struggling and moving body with two massive paws encircling each shoulder. The injuries thus inflicted within a span of a few seconds are mostly fatal and the man, the paragon of animals, instantly reverts two million years back to a defenceless prey, crumpled to the earth with a collosal weight upon him. Till the big cat realises its mistake of having caught something it does not require and leaves the kill, it is all over for the poor chap. The attack is definitely accomplished in an error of man being mistaken for a legitimate prey. To make it more clear a tiger's killing is culminated in a rapid sequence of events as he launches himself at the unseen object, the victim falls on the ground, and before his agonized screams issue from the throat, there come the *dhup-dhup-dhup* sounds as his body is shaken and relentlessly beaten against the earth and next moment, passed under the mighty weight upon him the victim is already dead. This accidental killing of man helps the tiger overcome his generations bred reluctance to attack man and it may at times induce an individual tiger to include human beings amongst his prey, or even convert him into a habitual man-eater.

From 1976 to 1987, sugarcane tigers had let loose a reign of terror in Kheri district and a controversial number of twenty tigers, most of them living in sugarcane fields had switched to man-eating. Fortunately, the number of confirmed and persistent man-eaters were very small.

Unfortunately, the response to this bizzare problem was one of over-reacting by the forest authorities. In their hurry to get over with it, an almost indiscriminate killing of tigers was resorted to. Probably no one had bothered to capture these tigers and transfer them to zoos. Billy Arjan Singh was among the leading conservationists to allege that several non man-eaters too had been eliminated in their killing spree. But it always happens. The innocent creatures are normally the first ones to pay the price for the follies of their wise cousins.

The traditional causes assigned for the birth of a man-eater are: insufficiency of food, failing age, incurable and permanent wounds or a faulty denture. They hamper the movements of a tiger and prevent him from securing his natural prey, but in case of sugarcane tiger, the situation is entirely different.

There was no shortage of natural food in this region and the area contains a good stock of prey species. The confirmed man-eaters that were being killed were later found to be animals having no apparent causes to turn to man-eating. None of them was old, no one carried a permanent wound or a faulty denture. All of them were able-bodied, healthy tigers. Then what had prompted them to take to man-eating?

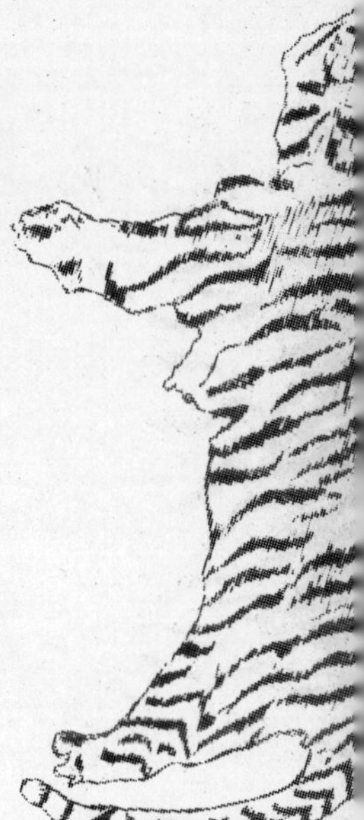

A conservative school of thought maintains that tigers have a musk-like odour which is easily discerned from a distance by the wild animals. In the jungle, the scent is not that effective because it is absorbed by the thick vegetation and often over-powered by the smell of aromatic plants. But in the open, it spreads faster and when a tiger is in the area, the wild game that stray away from the jungle to browse on crops, sense it quickly and stay away from the tiger zone. The rest of the animals move out from there. So the predatory beast faces a natural paucity of food. In the event, it is only the domesticated cattle, which admittedly have a dulled olfactory sense and weakened defence reflexes, and generally fail to catch the scent, which end up as the big cats meal.

In a revealing study on the Chitwan National Park in Nepal made by American biologist M. Sunquist in 1981, it was found that the daily food requirement of a tigress was 5 to 7 kgs and that of a tiger was 7 to 9 kgs. Discounting the inedible part of the carcasses and the loss of some meat to scavengers, it was estimated that the annual requirement of a female was 2,800 kgs to 3,600 kgs and that for a male was 3,300 to 4,000 kgs. On the basis of this and using certain established estimates, it was calculated that the crude biomass (or live weight of prey) available to tigers was between 3,500 kgs and 5,600 kgs per square mile.

This pertains to the availability of natural prey as the studies were conducted in a forest, but when it comes to the farm tigers, the availability as well as requirements certainly become different. But unfortunately, no such serious study has ever been undertaken in Dudhwa or in the Terai regions of north India, where the farm tigers are fairly common. The prey available to farm tigers is not their customary prey and the percentage of their customary prey that comes out of the jungle vis-a-vis the percentage of non-conventional prey (in the form of pets, etc.) is mostly lower. And in juxtaposition to this difference, the percentage of such farm tigers turning into ardent cattle-lifters and subsequently, man-eaters should also be higher. But all this is mere conjencture as no such exhaustive study has ever been conducted of such a mundane thing as the variation in the prey list of a jungle tiger and a farm tiger.

Investigations prove that man-eating is more frequent in females than in males. For, after having laid the cubs, the movements of the tigress become severely restricted. She spends most of her time in nursing her little ones and this bondage gives rise to the most prominent problem of food. Nature has installed a characteristically solitary temperament in the tiger. The creature is an individualist. Like lions, whose social organisations and group hunting techniques generally ensure security and food for both the old and incapacitated members and a nursing mother who during this period always relies on the kills made by other members of the pride and instead of going for hunting, she rightfully affords to take care of the new progeny. The social interdependence is so great that besides sharing kills, lionesses of a pride suckle other cubs as well as their own.

In contrast to this, the situation with the tiger is quite different. He has no provider of food to depend upon and in times of trouble, whether old, injured or incapacitated, the tiger must rise and go for hunting, or else die a treacherous death by starvation.

The tribe bonds being absent, the litter-rearing tigress thus, stands a big chance of falling prey to this unseemly habit. It is evidently the difficulty in finding food for their young ones, that normally initiates females in this bad habit.

However, a few experts argue that their attacks on human beings often cease to take place as soon as their cubs become sufficiently grown up to fend for themselves. But somehow this hypothesis does not go with sound reasoning. We must remember that the habits picked up in the initial stages of schooling from their mother become indoctrinated in the minds of the cubs as a gospel truth that has to be followed throughout the life. Under such circumstances, the mother may later abandon man-eating but the cubs will definitely carry on the legacy of their mother.

In the early eighties, five sugarcane tigresses were identified as man-eaters. The middle of the decade saw a conspicuous increase in the number of man-eating tigers in this area. The authorities had no answer but to believe that this vice was taken up by young cubs from their mother, born in the sugarcane and were now finding man an easy prey were perpetuating this habit.

A thorough analysis showed that indeed these cubs had started the very first day of their lives in the close proximity of man. Some studies put the degree of this association as being 30 to 60 per cent of total human sightings by the tiger cubs. The experience gained by this informal association removes their initial shyness of man and their aberrant behaviour, as we term it, was indeed the fall-out of socio-ecological conflict.

Every predator is basically shy of human beings as man is not their natural prey. The tremendous evolution of this anthropod ape which made him walk upright, live in groups, talk loudly, wear colourful clothes, go about his vocation in the day and his intelligent reactions, automatically forced nature to drop his name from the predator's list of prey. This had happened over two to three million years ago and since then, as the habitat requirement of the two species differed, man went out of the jungle to settle as a farmer. He, thus, ceased to be the prey of tiger. But we must not forget that in man, the senses of self- preservation have been diluted over the ages by scientific development, and the tiger, in his position as a master predator, can prey on any other species. And when the tiger is forced by circumstances and hunger to wander in human areas, he can prove potentially dangerous to them. He can acquire man-eating traits at any age and, like cattle-killing, it may also become a tradition passed on from parents to the younger generation. The off spring of such tigers follow the example of their parents, for the life of a tiger, or for that matter any animal, is not only an aggregate of its instincts, a transference of the practice and habits of countless ancestors, but in truth it is altered and moulded by the challenging circumstances and parental traditions through the experience a tiger cub acquires in their association.

Killing human beings may be an easy task, but its consequences are highly punishing and now as at this stage the tigers *viz.* man-eaters, deal with the extremely intelligent species of prey so they too themselves develop into wily and devilishly clever characters. They always cover a much larger territory and travel deeper into the sugarcane crops, than the normal tigers of the jungle. Here, the customary food of the tiger is naturally scarce but the basic reason for the exceptional restlessness of the man-eater is his limitation of feeding upon the human kill. Rarely do such tigers get an opportunity to feed upon their kill twice, as under the normal course of events, they do with their customary kill in the jungle. They usually feed on it only once and by the next day, the remains are generally reclaimed by the victims' kin and removed from the scene. Moreover, the edible contents or the food value of a human kill is not sufficient to appease a tiger's hunger. This keeps the tiger almost half-starved and encourages him for a constant search of the next meal.

At the same time, the shyness from man compels it to maintain as much distance as possible between itself and the spot of his latest human kill.

It is difficult to put down an inflexible rule pertaining to the behaviour of the tiger. Some experts right in the 19th century appeared inclined to assign certain reactions to the tiger in his encounter with humans. And the trend is still followed.

It bears remembering that in that period about 40 per cent of land area in the Indian peninsula consisted of forests and a tiger had a verdant habitat to operate in.

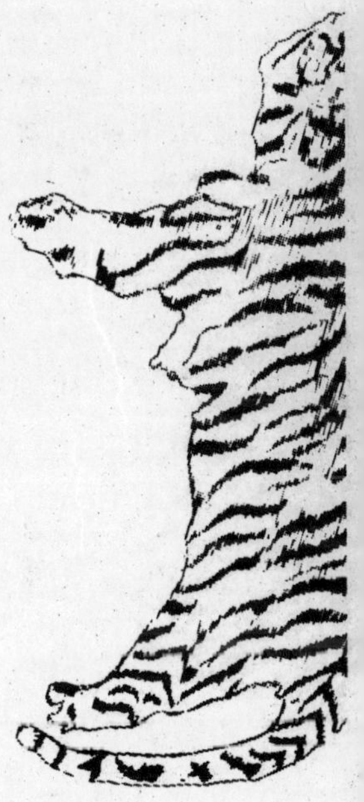

Their prime homes always remained undisturbed and inaccessible between jungles and pockets of cultivation, there existed naturally huge buffer areas of scrub and grass. Thus both the species, *viz.* humans and tigers, had ample room to avoid each other. It will not be an exaggeration to say that in those days, despite the raging hunting seasons, many tigers, still lived in peace and died a natural death without ever setting eyes on a single human being in their life. Now the situation has reversed, and the sugarcane tiger comes across a much larger number of humans than his wild co-tenants. As already suggested, tigers living in biotically disturbed forest complexes are actually harassed beasts, their constant and extraordinary frequent association with man has given them an entirely different kind of manner. A few tigers react against the ravages of their ecosystem while others avoid them, whereas a few take it casually and still a few tigers react timidly. They display a great variety in their personality and approach pertaining to their behaviour with man. An intense compulsion is required before a tiger embarks upon the alien diet of human flesh, for after all, nature has made them the predators of the highest degree.

They possess the disastrous capability to injure a man, leave alone their teeth and claws, they can do this even by a sheer rasping of their tongue upon his body. The numerous pointed sheaths which cover the tongue prick into one's finger like so many rigid pins, and are well-suited for the licking of thick layers of skin and the bones of animals. No beast of prey is so exceedingly well-equipped and so specialised as tigers are for their particular role in life. It is quite ironical that all the body weaponry of the tiger, meant to subdue and tear apart hard and rough wild prey is almost wasted when he attacks and kills a man, for only a small per cent of the killing force is put into use. On the other hand, it is also surprising that despite so much of torment, they have still not reacted with even one per cent of their total capacity to destroy.

Amidst the Terai region, Lakhimpur Kheri district has no long history of man-eaters operating here. Extending from generations past, it had remained mercifully free from this menace. I am of the opinion that after India's independence and specially in the last decade, many man-eaters have been products of biotic disturbances, for many of its areas have been thoughtlessly ravaged by the ploughers and harvesters. Several contemporary wildlife experts have already dwelt on this subject and here I do not feel the need to cite cases of man-eating by sugarcane tigers and account for their explanation. One must acknowledge that despite the odds being heavily stacked against them, tigers are virtually practicing great restraint. I have known of a few cases which show that even under the most provocative circumstances, they refrain from devouring human flesh.

On May 3, 1990, when I was camping in the Bhujia farm of M. P. Singh, I received the news that the previous night, a fish-poacher was killed by a tiger on the bank of Suheli river. Losing no time, I went over to investigate at the spot of the occurrence with my companion Rajesh Gupta who had once been an active member of my anti-poaching squad. The tiger's victim, named Ikram Mohammed of Palia Kalan, was a notorious fish-poacher of the area and for many years he had been earning his living through illegal fishing done in the Dudhwa Park. Earlier his gang hunted by day-light, but strict vigilance by the forest patrol had greatly hampered their activities and finally compelled them to carry out their operations by midnight.

The previous night (May 2), Ikram, accompanied by four fishermen had gone out on his usual fishing expedition. They stretched their nets in the river Suheli and waited on the banks. They had no idea that just a few seconds before their arrival, a tigress had struck a spotted deer right at the place they chose to bivouac, and before she could commence eating, she was disturbed by their arrival. To avoid them, she had dragged the kill to a close-by cluster and was now sitting only a few meters behind the poachers. The tigress was in no mood to advertise her presence. She expected rather the men to clear off soon and enable her to eat the kill at ease, but sometime later, Ikram left the banks to ease himself. As his misfortune would have it, he went straight in to the bush where the tigress was sitting to guard her kill. The man must have collided with the tigress who as a reflex action, executed just a slap on the man's face which dislocated the man neck and killed him instantly. Then, displaying her resentment, she caught hold of the man's shoulders and dragged him into another thicket. There she left the body but made no attempt to eat it. The poachers were scared out of their wits and, abandoning their catch, decamped with all the speed they could muster.

Later, I did an intensive examination of the spot, and found that the predator was a tigress of average size. The pugmarks also showed that she had been in no mood to enter into a confrontation with man and at least twice she had changed her position from one bush to another to avoid the men, who were inadvertently loitering close to her. But when finally the situation worsened and in blatant defiance of a tiger's domain, a man entered the very bush where she had been sitting, she had no option left but to surprise the intruder. The evidence also indicated that later, the tigress had come back to her kill and had devoured a hearty meal. It was by sheer chance that she had already procured her normal diet, otherwise this incident could have marked the beginning of yet another man-eater's career and the beast could have proved no exception to the inviolable rule that man-eaters are generally created by the interference of the human race.

Under normal circumstances, the tiger is a gentleman and a noble natured beast. He kills only for food and never for want or lust. Only the mother tigress, with her half-grown cubs may become an exception to this rule. She is known to indulge in extra killings specially at the time when she teaches her young ones the art of hunting. The cubs are supposed to go about the process of stalking, attacking and slaying, exactly in the way of a tiger, since they have to live by hunting only. In their normal play. It is interesting to observe how the cubs crouch and leap at each other and at times catch hold of each other's neck. Actually it is their carnivorous instinct which induces them to practice, albeit unconsciously, the elements of their craft. The tigress trains them how to break the *vertebrae* of the victims neck. The mother tigress who takes her cubs for hunting in the field, disables her prey to the extent that it cannot escape. She then encourages her cubs to take a share in the killing. This particular time is full of problems for the villagers.

In the beginning, the young tigers are naturally not well versed in the art of killing. They are ineffectual killers, and are liable to commit several errors. They always improperly handle their kill and generally in the process, injure themselves and at times quite badly. If the kill is thoroughly incapacitated, they often feed on the living animal and do not bother to terminate its existence before they embark upon the feast. The killing is actually a cumbersome business. It needs strength and cunning and also demands considerable labour. In their inefficiency, the young tigers try to satisfy their hunger first and in the easiest possible way. They tear out the chunks of food and gorge them. This is not a pleasant act to watch. The pray is often partly eaten before it is finally dead. The animal bellows and struggles to escape even as its entrails are pulled out and hunks of flesh are torn from its rump. A sight of such a gruesome death may disturb human sensibilities, but it is immaterial in the animal world. However this is something the tigress does not want. To correct such kinds of mistakes, the tigress consistently remains with her cubs and demonstrates to them at the earliest opportunity, the proper style and secrets of killing the prey.

With this, the frequency of prey killing also increases. There is an indispensable lesson learnt by the cubs, at times at the exceptionally great cost of cattle.

From 1984 to 1986, no less than five mother tigresses were known to have been training their cubs in the sugarcane fields, threatening harvesters of dire reprisals. They were active in between the area ranging from Pallia to Sampoornanagar and one of them was stationed at the outskirts of Paraspur Village.

I have already said that high reproductive potential is reflected by farm tigers. Mamman Khan had once shot a tigress near Makanpur village which carried as many as seven foetuses in her womb. I have also known of two authentic cases in which the litter of five cubs had taken place. Still, the carnivorous population does not seem to register a very significant increase mainly because the infant mortality rate, whether in the jungle or on the farm, seems very high. The cubs being the lowest in the hierarchy and still not proficient in the techniques of their tribe, naturally become the first casualty against the critically lowered number of prey species. Climatic conditions, drought or inundation, food competition, and of course the adverse local situations and above all the inter-species tensions, which in the event of food shortage, normally result in the elimination of weak rival animals, always and infallibly must first tell upon the cubs, that is why the chances of one of the multiple cubs surviving till adulthood are rated as 20 to 40 per cent. This factor chiefly keeps their number within the restricted limits.

Every year, on the auspicious day of *Sarva Pitra Amavasya*, the princely family of Singahi generally sets free a stud bull to court with the cows. In the winter of 1988, soon after the bull was released in the field, it was attacked by a mother tigress. She drove him towards her cubs who were waiting in a nearby cane field. In a quick leap, she almost mounted the bull and incapacitating him and injuring him with her grievous blows, she drove him almost riding to her half-grown cubs. The cubs in their impatience and confidence provided by the presence of their mother, engaged the bull in a fight on the outskirts of Bela village. Eye-witnesses later told me that at first, the tigress had left the bull and stood at a short distance changing her position from time to time to get a better view of the efforts of the cubs, but they were not big enough to hold the stud bull by themselves. The tigress in order to disable the bull further, once again attacked him. Meanwhile, a rescue force of villagers arrived on the scene. Their shouts and a few blank shots fired in the air disheartened the tigress, who took her cubs and retreated somewhere in the sea of sugarcane crops.

The bull had survived the fight and later recovered from his injuries, but a cub who was known to have received a bad stab from the bulls horns was reported to have died at the outskirt of Maliniya village, that stands some two kilometers West of Bela.

Now, within the span of a decade, no less than 120 persons have been killed by the cane-dwelling tigers. On the other hand, the unofficially sponsored statistics are staggering to contemplate, for this amounts to over 250 victims. During the same decade under review, it was stated that at least 300 plus livestock had fallen victim to sugarcane tigers. How many more could have been added in this eternal war raged by the tigers is anyone's guess. Many instances may not have been brought to the notice of the authorities and thus not included in the list. I must make it clear that all the men were not killed by man-eaters, and how could they, when all the confirmed man-eaters had already been destroyed either by the foresters or had been poisoned to death by farmers? Why were humans still being killed by tigers—simply because we did not want to leave them alone in peace.

We must acknowledge that tigers alone are not responsible for the trouble. The villagers also sometimes tend to invite trouble by themselves.

The conditions may have changed, but we have still not learnt to co-exist with our wild life. In largely unfounded and generation-bred ignorant convictions, we generally deal with wild animals with two basic reactions, either we are scared of them, or we want to harm them. What we lack is the art to avoid them and tackle them, with equable and placid temper. No animal is innately evil, which is best exemplified by the sedately ignorant attitude of the mighty elephants towards human beings even at close quarters. No tiger strikes at a man by choice. In the general course of things, tigers are extraordinarily retiring beasts; they display greater tolerance for humans beings than the latter do for them. They are actually the pressing conditions that create the wicked characters. Such conditions, in turn, are created by the expansionist, self-centered and callous humans.

To support my case, I can do no better than to cite two instances of how the tigers are tormented and the essential tranquility of their nature is broken. They are badly harassed and provoked and we know that when a predator is pushed against the wall, his reactions hardly leave any scope for his tormentors to escape. Even a minor reaction on his part can be fraught with terribly devastating results.

Way back in the early 80's, Yogesh and I had been engaged in conducting a second field investigation of the man-eating problem in Lakhimpur-Kheri District which had by then assumed magnified proportions. One day during our stay at Gola township, we learnt of yet another tragedy which had happened. Some 15 miles to the south of Katna reserve forest is situated a small village named Aheri. At the outskirts of this village, a number of bamboo clusters grow closely set on the west side, giving the place a look of a natural bamboo grove. On the fine morning of July, 2, 1979, some village herdsmen out on their routine work came across the pugmarks of a tiger near the bamboo grove. Anxious to learn more about the animal, they went inside the cluster and soon located the striped form of the tiger resting amidst the thick bamboo shoots. It appeared that the animal had come near the village in search of food. And as its pugmarks showed, he had wandered around the settlement for the entire night, but without success.

Finally at day break, he had found it safe to retire in the cool and remote shade of the bamboo cluster. The excited yet scared men retreated hastily and called out to their fellow folk. Immediately, a mob turned up on the spot and all the men, women and children were impatient to have a glimpse of the beast. Among the keen watchers was a local *pandit* named Amarnath who had also carried here his 12 bore DBBL shotgun. He was a sly poacher himself and finding a good opportunity, he set his mind to bag the tiger. He moved ahead and cautiously advanced up to two metres of the spot where the tiger sat concealed. As he looked around to find the animal and aim the gun, the tiger suddenly emerged from his hide-out. In the split second he sprang upon the *pandit* who did not have any time to even move from his position. The man fell down on the ground, his gun being thrown away. The tiger mauled him and stood for some moments upon his prostrate body, his jaws dripping with blood. Faced with this hideous sight, the rest of the men yelled at the top of their lungs to scare the tiger away. At this, the startled animal turned and again retreated into his hide-out. The incapacitated man was lifted and rushed to the village for whatever medical attention could be rendered.

The men spread out, surrounding the bamboo thicket with whatever weapons they had in their hands. A message was sent by a runner to the local police post and two armed constables duly arrived on the scene. The terrified villagers narrated the entire incident to them and indicated the spot where the tiger was supposed to be hiding. The matter was then handed over to the custodians of law to deal with as they deemed fit. The policemen, feeling important, issued quick instructions much as the unfortunate *pandit* had taken upon himself to deal with the tiger. The villagers were asked to collect dry cane leaves and scatter them in abundance around the thicket. Then the green cluster was set on fire. The two policemen took position at a safe distance with their guns aimed at the inferno. All of a sudden, and with an amazing display of agility, the tiger sprang out of the grove and bolted blindly in one direction. By a singular stroke of misfortune, another bystander, Harkaran Bajpai stood in the tiger's path. Inevitably, he was felled by the tiger and was pinned down by the sheer weight of the animal. His face and chest bore the brunt of the tiger's incisors and blood gushed out of the wounds. As the tiger vanished, the custodians of law, denied the opportunity of firing the famed shots, took the poor man to a nearby dispensary where he later died. The earlier victim, Amarnath, was lucky to survive.

The second instance, no less tragic, is more recent. In the winter of 1990, at a village near Sampurnanagar, some villagers happened to see a tiger who was crossing their path through the sugarcane field. The tiger was going his own way and upon seeing the crowd of passers by, he immediately got behind a *peepal* tree and concealed himself in a bush, but the men had already spotted him. Excited as they were, they sent a message to their fellow beings in the village, to come and enjoy the sight of a tiger. Soon a large number of people turned up to see the animal. The tiger had become nervous and unable to move, and was left with no option, so he sat concealed and motionless. The villagers lingered on and their numbers constantly swelled, expressing the vehemence of their individual patterns of whims. The crowed shouted, clapped, threw stones and abused the tiger, daring it to come out but the tiger did not leave his hide-out. Finally the curious onlookers started closing in upon the bush to get a better view. The animal now turned jittery and broke out of the foliage to escape. Just in the very nick of the moment, a teenaged boy Rajesh Kumar happened to come in the way of the tiger who just swept him aside with his right paw. The casual slap of the bounding tiger proved fatal for the unfortunate boy who collapsed right on the spot and died.

Some octogenarian inhabitants of the area, say that for years, they had known that tigers infested these jungles but it was rare to see them, unless they systematically sought them. They categorically assert that the number of tigers has not increased that much, but on the contrary, it is the jungles which have shrunk by more than half. And that is the crux of the problem. The responsibility for this lies squarely on the shoulders of humans.

Man's quest for more land and food has made wild game scarce. The tiger has been driven out of his natural habitat and compelled to seek a new home. It is incredible to understand how marvelously, even after being put to terribly hazardous life and persecution, he has adapted himself to the antipodal change of his primeval ecosystem into which his tribe has been autogenetically integrated. For no fault of his, he is termed cantankerous and rapscallion.

Man continues to impinge upon his natural territory which is already receding under the heavy pressure of cattle grazing and wood poaching. The growth of natural forests is being retarded as a result of which the population of his natural prey is decimated. Thus, the regional number of tigers may become incompatible with the food supply of the area and they are liable to involuntarily interact more and more with the human life-style. Their encounters with humans will become more frequent however reluctant such a situation might be for both. Such tigers having accepted the farms as their new and complete environment, do not return to the jungles again, they do not even take to the ecological belt of their previous ecosystem. In the event of interspecies tension or the harassed conditions, they rather penetrate deeper into the cane country.

Finally, in their wayfaring, they cross over the customary range of their prey and turn solely to the human settlement for food. An example of this can be cited in the periodical appearance of three tigers at a small isolated picnic spot of Chinhat jungle near my own metropoliton city of Lucknow which is at a distance of no less than 150 miles away from the closest Terai jungle belt of Bahraich and Lakhimpur Kheri District. It is actually a fall out of this great migrations of tigers as the constant stretch of sugarcane belt provide an ample room for their vandalism. It is not surprising that moving through them secretly and unnoticed they even manage to reach Lucknow where they eventually meet their ignominous end at the hands of man. The last tiger was shot dead in December 1989, only three miles away from my house of Indra Nagar Colony.

First they take to goat, dog and poultry killing, then on to cattle. After that as they get used to the clatter, and hubbub of human settlements, they shun their shyness of man who is then liable to become the next logical target.

Since the situation is different, we will have to give a discount to the tiger. These tigers, who have been killed for man-eating, should be accepted as having actually died in the defence of their heritage against the plunderings of man!

I have been fortunate to utilise the wealth of knowledge produced in the works of several celebrated hunters, naturalists, scientists, conservationalists and wildlife managers. I have not cited their individual references but I hope that the learned scholars will forgive me for the use of material as well as any misinterpretations and simplifications of their researches and ideas and the information incorporated therein.

Conclusion

In conclusion, I wish to say that every wildlifer who writes a book relating to his own experience and adventure does so with an apparent intention and once you have finished reading this book, you must have perceived my original motive. With the risk of some repetition I would say that it constantly emphasizes the conservation of wild animals. The subject of wildlife cannot be restricted by the national boundaries, for the animals freely move from one country to the other. Birds migrating from Siberia and elsewhere cross over many countries, thus all the responsibility of their conservation cannot be claimed only by one country or organisation. It becomes the duty of mankind to assume the responsibility of such an important natural heritage of world. Many organizations of developing countries have generously donated a tremendous amount of money to various organisations of the third world to safeguard the interest of this precious treasure. Wild life is therefore, an international subject.

However, in Indian conditions, the priorities of conservation operations don't appear to have achieved their target. The forests are still being felled in the name of development and the great marshes and ponds which harbour the migratory birds virtually in thousands are still giving way to paddy fields. The construction of new factories and their colonies for labourers and continuous bubbling smoke have completely changed the character of those primeval landscape which in only the recent past were spacious green belts and teeming with a tremendous variety of wildlife. It is particularly noticeable in Terai and the decline of animal there is very marked.

In this book, I have striven hard to impart some information about poaching and I am perfectly well aware that there are many more methods that are contributing to the decline of game all over India. The methods described earlier in this context were the outcome of my own initiative and experience. Being an avid reader myself, I would like to remind the discerning reader that in addition to the afore mentioned ways of poachers there also exist the following time tested methods, which as usual differ from region to region depending upon geographical terrain.

A little changed version of archery is a large cross-bow. It is fitted on the ground to kill dangerous animals. Several records of natural history describe this method used by native hunters to dispose off tigers, leopards and bears etc. In British India, they were regarded as vermins and their skins were brought to district collectors to claim rewards. This bow is made of double bamboo fitted into a solid stock. It's string is made of thick rope a short javelin like arrow furnished with a barbed point and richly coated with saturated poison is pulled on the cross-bow. The united strength of three to four persons just barely helps to draw the strings to lock the weapon which is laid on the ground and is crossed through the supposed path of big cats and is fastened to the peg firmly fixed in the earth. As the passing animal drags the cord along, the arrow releases with a tremendous force, striking at the beast with a serious thrust and gets embedded into its body. The big cats are often known to be knocked down by its force. They hardly move for about hundred yards from the spot before the virulent poison makes them drop dead. In the same manner, loaded guns of both variety. The muzzle loading and the breach loading are also fitted on the ground. Their trigger is tied to the cord and the passing animals are riddled with bullets.

Tiger and leopards are snared in a variety of traps, the most popular amongst them is a large cage made of thick bamboo that are tied firmly together with a stout rope. In the inner compartment, a buffalo calf or a goat is kept to serve as a bait. Its trap door is so contrived that as soon the cat enters the cage. It falls and closes, caging the beast inside. The mighty feline is reduced to utter helplessness is speared by hunters with impunity.

Bachandi is a common plant of Terai and central India, it's roots have a toxic effect poacher's grind it's, dry roots throw the powder in small water ponds of jungle. Thirsty birds drinking this water temporarily fall unconscious. The state sets in about three to four minutes after the intake and lasts for about half an hour. The poachers watch their movement and as they fall they come out of their hide-out and collect them. Many of the variety are killed to be eaten while others as they recover are caged and sold in the market.

Peacocks and cranes are very easily caught. In the atmosphere of still air, due to their heavy bodies they are unable to beat their wings for long flight and become fatigued within a short time. The poachers make a good use of such times. They post a few men at strategic points where the birds are expected to take refuge. Then the beat starts, and the birds with heavy beating of their wings leave their perches to escape. On the way they meet stave waving, shouting and stone throwing men. This makes them deflect their flight from one direction to another and keeps them in the air, with no opportunity granted even for a second to alight on any one tree and rest. Thus, subjected to assiduous flights their energies quickly wane, and they fall completely exhausted on the ground only to meet a treacherous end of their life. Male peacocks with long tails are more vulnerable than none tailed females or young ones.

Wild cranes are caught with the help of domesticated cranes. Poachers leave their pet cranes to peck amongst them who get mixed up and bring them along into man's ambush. Here, they are easily noosed and sold to meat vendors.

This method has been largely held responsible for the rapid depletion in population of Siberian cranes. Just a few years back over two hundred birds migrated into the Ghana bird Sanctuary while in January 1993 barely five birds were sighted. International union of conservation for natural resources, took it seriously and the investigations revealed that their poaching by tribals in Iran, Afghanistan and Pakistan was rampant. While on their flight to India they cross over these countries and the tribals there on seeing their flocks release their pet cranes who fly along and lure them to alight on their land where they are wantonly massacred.

This poaching alarmingly tells that all political parties and their subsequently formed governments must muster up the courage and display some risk-taking potential of their vote blocks and immediately take up stringent steps to implement the law more firmly and enforce preservation otherwise our rapidly disappearing feathered and furred fauna will soon be extinct. Precisely I visualise, by the beginning of 21st century, we will be destitute of all birds and animals.

The combined onslaught of development population boom, industrialization and many other factors, have penned the animals into a very narrow space, probably to the detrement of their natural vigour and development.

I personally feel, that Indian democracy and the complexity of its political scenario is an intense ban for wild-life as a result of which one another menace of terrorism has recently emerged to add its toll to the destruction of wild animals, the supporters of this ideology, apparently to escape the hands of law, seek their shelter in the jungles. The genesis of this problem lies in the Indian society which is divided in to several dichotomous units like rich and poor, religious fundamentalism, blackmail of pressure groups, grievance situations identity crises, regionalism, casteism, and above all, the elite politicians and their electors, the ignorant masses. All these factors breed more discontent than satisfaction and taking advantage of it, the twisted policies of neighbouring countries to destabilize India by supplying arms and moral support, also manifests into innumerable problems. They may become a material for debate. On the intellectual plane, with fancy names such as dialectical understanding of revolutionary situation, terrorism as a weapon in politics, gun as an argument or the publicity value of terror, no concrete plan is designed to curtail such factors and no law is full heartedly implemented by the political heroes to crush it. Now this phenomenon has assumed magnified dimensions and the hench men of this sub human ideology are dispersed throughout Indian jungles under the name of various organizations like cyanide capsule, guerilla fighter, naxalites, commando forces and liberation armies etc. they are armed with a high quality of rifles such automatic kalashnikov, 47 and kala-n-kov 56. In their attempt to force government to retreat, they are known to have done worse type of killings than even the hardest of the native poachers could have imagined. Only recently in Bakeyganj area of Lakhimpur-Kheri district 16 wild boars riddled with the AK 47 bullets were found, some rigger-happy militant had evidently done a bit of target shooting on them and left them there. No one cared to report the incident, for the natives were rather happy to get so much of flesh free of cost. Death and destruction to such men are not mere threats but a part of a programme of actions and

when mankind is nothing for them, then where do the poor animals stand. They indiscriminately massacre every type of wildlife with a complete disregard for their number, sex and age.

In truth, when we see all these factors in totality, there appears no force strong enough to break these problematic characters and this dichotomy again paves the way for further complexities. Millions of poor Indians living on the periphery of parks just do not know what their natural heritage is. They look at the forest and its animals just as a source of food, for after all, for them it is a strange thing that the people with hunting in their blood for hundreds of years are suddenly denied their rights and have to do without its taste. Majority of them may be chump headed illiterates, but they do not forget that they live in and make the largest democracy of the world and the animals cannot exist without their will. They have been made for their stomach and that must remain so. I am pained to tell that a political contestant in a constituency near Dudhwa Park fought and won the election on the assurance that he would get the already depleted cover of national park thrown open for the masses to collect fire wood free of cost. The demagogic and histrionic approach of politicians during elections is more for gathering support rather than trying to understand the true nature of people's problems.

The anomaly lies in the qualifications required for the government servants for members of legislative assembly and members of Parliament. For a government job, one needs to be at least a graduate, where as to contest an election one needs an automatic qualification which comes to him in time and that is the age of 25 years for legislative assembly and 30 years for parliament. It has nothing to do with the literacy or mental level of the candidate.

Many public figures are not enlightened by the fact that in Indian conditions where primitive ignorance is heavy on the minds of people if such assurances are given and in case even mindlessly applied it will be a near disaster, the complete Sanctury will cease to exist within no time under the mounting pressure of demography.

This is there because the subject of wildlife is still regarded as something secondary, the greater budget allocations, staff recruitment and other priorities will naturally go to other departments whereas the holocast on ecology must be opposed with determination and political will and necessarily be linked at the ideological-plane. Its allied concepts such as forestry, social foresting, conservations, desilting etc., must strictly be taken up.

The population is growing at an enormous rate, more land and more food is needed, there is no viable solution to meet this problem, and almost every plan has failed to check it and when more than 40% of the child population of this country will reach the reproductive age, the population explosion is bound to take place. However, immediately, again the shrinking edges of forest which now constitute barely 8% of India, landmass are greedily eyed as the answer to all their needs. Inept and impromptu moves on the part of myopic planners may provide a temporary relief by settling down a segmental population but very soon it begins to tell heavily upon the health of the ecology and becomes counter productive as it retards almost all the growth and development.

We must not look only for the immediate solution but make our plans with an eye for the future of this planet in a greater respect of time and space. In the Indian context, and particularly in the context of Terai, firstly over 20 thousand hectare land of forests that is being illegally occupied and ploughed by farmers must be reclaimed with stringent measures, and the forest there be regrown. The tribals have now ceased to be the part of ecology.

Tharus, Boxa and Khasis who at some parts are still living inside the forest are damaging to wild habitats rather than being an asset to preserve them. Precisely, they have become an important subject for the government's development plans. Providing them a school and dispensary is alright. But with an all round development several concrete buildings have sprung up in the core areas of the jungle. This is paving the way for business and commercialization of their tribal art and skills with the result that the government's so called development is actually culminating in a severe deterioration of ecology.

The tribals must be brought out from the interiors of the forest with new schemes and subsidies designed for their welfare. The economic development of natives living on forest fringes should be closely guarded because they are the first and the last individuals who matter foremost for the success of any scheme of conservation. Without native support, no flora and fauna can survive. New audio-visual programmes pertaining to the importance of wildlife and nature should be shown amongst such masses. It will help to enlighten them about the measures of conservation.

The most important is that the sugarcane cultivation must be translocated out of the forest land because it helps to turn a normal tiger into a man-eater. Major research projects to genuine non-governmental organizations (NGOs) should also be encouraged because they give an objective report, while departmental reports often hide their shortcomings and are prone to be subjective. More forest corridors should be regenerated to adjoin separate forest blocks and the villagers should be shifted and provided with reasonable alternative sources of subsistence.

A moderate budgetary allocation is needed, which will help

to raise an adequate staff for an effective control and patrol of forests. Once we give back some part of the rightful land of wild animals, the extended habitat will enable them to move freely through corridors and this, to some extent will help to reduce the conflict that is so prominently emerging between man and his contestants of this planet. I am convinced that to save this precious natural heritage of India, every political expediency is worth the risk, for we have to save the very foundations of an incipient but emerging nation of orients.

Select Bibliography

1. Allen, Hugh: *The Lonely Tiger*, 1960.
2. Anderson, Kenneth: *Man Eaters and Jungle Killers*, 1961.
3. Bolton, M: Royal Chitwan National Park Management Plan— 1975-79, NEP/72/002, Project Working Documents No.2, UN DP/FAO/Kathmandu.
4. Boswell, K :'Scent Trails' and 'Poking' in Tiger, *Journal of Bombay Natural History Society; 54(2; 452-454)*, 1957.
5. Brader, A Dunbar: *Wild-Animals of Central India*, London 1923.
6. Burton, R.G.: *The Book of the Tiger*, 1933.
7. Burke, W.S: *The Indianfield Shikarbook*, 1908.
8. Corbett, Jim: *Man-Eaters of Kumaon*, 1944.
   The Temple Tiger and More Man-Eaters of Kumaon.
9. Dollman, G. and Brulace, J.: *Roweland Words Records of Big-game* (1935).
10. Gee, E.P. : *The Wild-Life of India*, 1964.
11. Holloway, C.W. Leyhausen P. and Ranjit Singh, M.K.: *Conservation of the Tiger in India*, IUCN, 1976.
12. Mc Dougal, C and Seinden Sticker, J.: *The Tigers of Mohan Khola*, 1976.
13. Mc Dougal, C.: *The Face of the Tiger*, 1977.
14. Mount Fort, G.: *Saving the Tiger.*
15. Prater, S.: *The Book of Indian-Animals*, 1948.
16. Powell, A.: *The Call of the tiger*, 1957.
17. Schaller, G. : *The Dear and the Tiger*, 1967.
    The Serengeti Lion, 1972.
18. Singh, A.: *Tiger Haven*, 1973. *Tiger ! Tiger!* 1984.

19. Sankhala, K.: *Tiger*, 1978.

20. Sunquist, M.E.: *The Movements and Activities of Tigers In Royal Chitwan National Park, Nepal*, Ph. D Thesis. 1979

21. Somerville, Augustus.: *The Home of the Man-Eater*, 1933 *The Passing of the Forest Gods.*

22. Thapar Valmiki: *Tiger, Portrait of a Predator*, Collins, London, 1986.

Cheetal: Journal of W.L. P.S. I. 1976, 78, 79, 80, 82,

India Today, 1986, 88, 89,

The Times of India, Delhi and Lucknow editions, 1984, 85, 86, 90, 91, 92, 93.

Scientific Names Of The Species Of Principal Animals, Birds And Reptiles

ASIAN ELEPHANT (*Elephant Maximus*) More compact than the African elephant. Most tractable. Famous for its services to mankind.

BAT, bearded sheath tailed Taphozous, Melanopogan.

Bat, fulvous frecit, Rousettus bechenaulti, all the three bats are fairly common in Indian peninsula and south east Asia.

BLACK BUCK (*Antelopa Cervicapra*) Handsome antelope on the verge of extinction.

BONNET MACAQUE, Macacaraaliatr.

CHITAL (Axis axis) Strongly spotted deer, weighing up to 200 Ibs. Favpirte prey of leopard.

Common Cobra, Naja naja.

Common Karait Bangarus Eaeruleus.

GAVIAL (*Gavialis Gangeticus*) Also known as the *gharial.* The most seriously endangered of India's crocodiles. Protected since 1972.

FISHING CAT (*Felis Viverrina*) Rare overall, but fairly common in the Himalayan Terai area.

GREY LANGUR (*Presbyti Entellus*) Long-tailed monkey, up to 40 lbs.

HOG DEER (*Axis Porcinus*) Solid-looking, short-legged deer. Up to 125 lb.

HYENA STRIPED ; *Hyena hyena.*

INDIAN FOX; *Vulpes bengalensis*, found in whole of India and is fairly common in the waste and scrub lands.

INDIAN MONGOOSE (*Herpestes Griseus*) A great killer of snakes and rats.

INDIAN TIGER (*Pantbera Tigris Tigris*) One of the seven sub-species of tiger which survive in the world. Some 3,000 now live in India's parks and reserves, where they are fully protected.

JACKAL (*Canis Aureus*) Fox-sized predator, common in Himalayan Terai.

LAMMERGEIER (*Gypaetus Brabatus*) Bearded vulture, with wingspan up to ten feet.

LARGE INDIAN CINET; *Viberra zibetha.*

LEOPARD (*Pantbera Pardu*) Three sub-species of leopard survive in India. All are now protected, but numbers have decreased alarmingly.

LION (African) *Pantheraleo.*

MARSH CROCODILE (*Crocodylus Palustris*). An endangered species which has disappeared from most of India. Also known as the mugger. Now legally protected, but still subject to poaching for its skin.

MONITOR LIZARD (*Varanus Monitor*) Agile lizard up to five feet long.

MUNTJAC (*Muntiacus Muntjac*) Barking deer, also known as the *kakar*. Up to 40 lbs.

NILGAI (*Boselaphus Tragocamelus*) Large, ungainly antelope which inhabits open plains.

PAINTED BAT, *Kerivoula picta.*

PEACOCK (*Pavo Cristatus*) The national bird of India.

PORCUPINE (*Hystrix Indica*) Preyed on by tigers and leopards. Up to 40 lb.

PYTHON (*Python Molorus*) Large snake fairly common in Himalayan Terai.

RAT SNAKE, *Pytas mucosus.*

RHESUS MONKEY (*Macaca Mulatta*) Favourite prey species of leopards. Up to 30 lbs.

RHINOCEROS. (Indian), *Rhinoceros unicornis.*

RED FOX; (*Vuples Vulpes*), a richly coloured fox with long silky brush.

SAMBAR (*Cervus Unicolor*) The largest deer in India. Up to 700 lbs.

SLOTH BEAR (*Melursus Ursinus*) Partially protected in India, Nepal and Sri Lanka, but still endangered.

SMOOTH INDIAN OTTER (*Lutra Perspicillata*) Fairly common in Terai.

SWAMP DEER (*Cervus Duvauceli*) An endangered species, now protected. The Dudhwa National Park is one of its main strongholds in Northern India. Weighs up to 500 lbs.

TIGER CIVET, *Prionodon Pardicolor.*

WILD BOAR, (*Sus Scrofa*) Favourite prey of the tiger.

WILD DOG *Cuon Alpinus.*

WOLF (*Canis Lupus*) Partially protected in India since 1972.

Index